MAGIC AND PAGANISM
IN EARLY CHRISTIANITY

MAGIC AND PAGANISM IN EARLY CHRISTIANITY

The World of the Acts of the Apostles

Hans-Josef Klauck

Translated by
Brian McNeil

FORTRESS PRESS   MINNEAPOLIS

Fortress Press edition 2003

This paperback edition published under license from T&T Clark Ltd.,
the Continuum International Publishing Group Ltd., London, U.K.

Translation copyright © 2000.

Authorized English translation of
Magie und Heidentum in der Apostelgeschichte des Lukas,
copyright © Verlag Katholisches Bibelwerk GmbH, Stuttgart 1996.

Cover image: Greek domestic altar from Italy;
located in the J. Paul Getty Museum (Los Angeles, California),
inv. #86.AD.598 (one of a pair); terracotta, c. 400–375 BCE;
photo © K. C. Hanson 2002.
Used by permission.

Cover design: Jessica Thoreson

ISBN: 0–8006–3635–X

09 08 07 06 05 04 03   1   2   3   4   5   6   7   8   9   10

*To my friends in South Africa,
where this study began*

CONTENTS

PREFACE

The German version of this book was very well received when it appeared in 1997, perhaps because the theme discussed here is relevant to our own day, although it has been little studied hitherto. For example, C. W. Stentschke wrote: 'Klauck takes the prize for writing the first monograph-length study of the Gentiles in Acts,' and: 'For the material he covers, the author provides a significant and exemplary study' (*Luke's Portrait of Gentiles*, 8). It was in fact necessary to reprint the German version in 1999, but unfortunately, for technical reasons, it was not possible to publish that as a genuine second edition. Happily, the situation with the English version is different: the text has been completely revised and the relevant secondary literature up to 1999 has been taken into consideration.

The following pages had their origin in a lecture in English which I gave at various places in South Africa in 1994 and which was subsequently published as an article (cf. *Neotestamentica* 28 [1994] 93–108). The German monograph, dedicated to my 'friends in South Africa', was written at a later date. Thus I am especially happy that this English translation and revision of my book is now published, since it is more accessible than the German text to the first hearers of my lecture. Brian McNeil has translated this book with his customary skill. I should like to express my gratitude to him and to the publishers, T&T Clark in Edinburgh.

Munich   HANS-JOSEF KLAUCK
January 2000

TRANSLATOR'S NOTE

Biblical translations are taken from the Revised Standard Version,
© 1973 by the Division of Christian Education of the National Council
of the Churches of Christ in the United States of America; sometimes
a more literal translation from the Greek New Testament is made, in
order to bring out the point of the author's arguments.

BRIAN MCNEIL

INTRODUCTION

Let us for a moment suppose that modern Europe were to witness the believers abandoning the Christian churches in order to venerate Allah or Brahma, to observe the commandments of Confucius or Buddha, to accept the fundamental principles of Shintoism; let us imagine a great congeries of all the races of the world, with Arabic mullahs, Chinese literary scholars, Japanese bonzes, Tibetan lamas, Hindu pandits preaching at one and the same time fatalism and predestination, the cult of ancestors and the adoration of the divinised ruler, pessimism and redemption through self-annihilation, while all these priests built temples in foreign styles in our cities and celebrated their various rites in them—this dream (which the future may perhaps one day see realised) would give us a rather accurate picture of the religious confusion which characterised the ancient world before Constantine.

These are the words of Franz Cumont, the Belgian historian of religion who is very well known (and justly renowned) in professional circles. They come from his classic work on the oriental religions in Roman paganism, in which he shows how oriental cults from Asia Minor, Syria, Egypt and Persia spread more and more in the Roman empire in the imperial period, and how astrology and magic took on a greater significance.[1] A whiff of the exotic and the mysterious attached to all of these, awakening curiosity. The attraction lay in the promise of an increase in the religiously mediated quality of life, something sought in vain in the traditional forms of religion.

The first edition of Cumont's book was published in 1906, i.e., at the beginning of the century which has just ended. One is almost tempted to ask whether Cumont enjoyed hidden prophetic gifts, since it was much too early for him to have heard the slogan of a multi-cultural and multi-religious society. Cumont's vision of the future awaits indeed its full realisation, but we have certainly taken steps in that direction. After the long phase of western Christendom with its relatively uniform culture, we now have the possibility of standing afresh in a situation that was a matter of everyday living for the first Christian generations. At the beginning, the Christian faith had to assert itself among the rival

---

[1] F. Cumont, *Les religions orientales dans le paganisme romain*, Paris 1906. German translation: *Die orientalischen Religionen im römischen Reich*, Darmstadt, seventh edn 1975, 178f.

religious views which literally competed with one another on the market-place for the favour of the public. We should make better use of the hermeneutical potential implicit in this analogy between the two situations, employing it to attain a deeper understanding both of earliest Christianity and of our own contemporary religious situation.

Are there passages in the New Testament which already reflect this process? The most likely place to look is in Luke's Acts of the Apostles,[2] which has many 'snapshots' that permit us to glimpse that distant, foreign, vivid and sometimes even dangerous world in which the Christian messengers of the first century after Christ moved. In the following chapters, we shall follow this process step by step. But before looking at the individual scenes, we shall first consider the foundations of the missionary programme of the book as a whole, which are established in its opening chapters.

I should like to make one point about terminology. As far as the phenomenon of 'magic' is concerned, its contours will become clearer in the course of our study of the texts. I am aware that concepts such as 'paganism, heathens, Gentile' remain problematic. The Old Testament and the New speak of the 'nations' when they refer to non-Jewish and non-Christian persons, and at most we find the expression 'unbelievers' (e.g., 1 Cor 14:23f.). 'Heathens' has negative connotations, as well as recalling the 'poor heathen children' portrayed by those well-meaning appeals in support of missionaries which now belong to the past. In the period with which we are concerned, the first century of the Common Era, these so-called pagans moved within their own religious systems, in subjective good faith. But what term are we to use, if we reject 'paganism'? If we speak of 'polytheism', we fail to include monotheistic tendencies within Greek and Roman philosophy which were critical of religion—tendencies which resonate in Paul's speech on the Areopagus (Acts 17). 'Religion' alone would be too general to be employed in the title of this book alongside 'magic', while the adjective in the term 'foreign religions' entails an evaluation from the standpoint of the one 'true religion'. I have therefore reluctantly decided to retain the traditional terminology, while pointing out how problematic it is.

---

[2] On this, see most recently D. Marguerat, 'Magie'; C. W. Stenschke, *Luke's Portrait of Gentiles*, esp. 133–243.

I

ESTABLISHING THE FOUNDATIONS (ACTS 1–2)

1. *Prologue and missionary programme (Acts 1:1–14)*

a. The dedicatory address

As with his Gospel (cf. Lk 1:1–4), Luke begins his second book with a brief prelude which adheres to the rules of the genre and is recognisably the introduction to a sequel: 'In the first book, O Theophilus, I have dealt with all that Jesus began to do and teach . . .' (Acts 1:1–3). It has often been demonstrated that Luke's Gospel prologue follows the conventions employed by professional hellenistic literary writers (especially in historical monographs, but in other special studies too) for dedicatory addresses; it is perhaps less well known that he does the same in the Acts of the Apostles. Specific, well-established patterns had been elaborated for the beginning of a new book in a work with two or more volumes. A glance at two Jewish authors will show that corresponding adaptations were made in Diaspora Judaism too. Thus Philo opens a monograph in which he discusses the Essenes with the following words: 'Our earlier investigation, O Theodotus, concerned the topic that every wicked person is a slave . . . The present study is concerned with a related theme . . . Here we intend to show that every virtuous person is free.'[1] Flavius Josephus makes the link to the continuation of his account in very similar terms: 'In the preceding book, most excellent Epaphroditus, I have demonstrated the venerable age of our people . . . Now I shall begin to refute the attacks of the others.'[2]

These two quotations suffice to indicate the characteristics of such a linking passage: the reference back to the first volume, the repetition of the address by name of the person to whom it is dedicated, and a look ahead to the contents of the new book. Luke takes up the first two of these points in Acts 1:1–3, where he summarises Jesus' ministry until his suffering and the Easter appearances, while he transposes the look ahead into the words which the risen Lord himself directly addresses to his disciples in v. 4. (In the Greek text, Luke makes this transition by passing unnoticeably, and with great skill, from the external perspective of his prologue into direct speech, bringing us as readers from the world of our daily lives into the narrated world of the text.) Since it is the risen

---

[1] *Quod omnis probus liber sit* ('That Every Virtuous Person is Free') 1.
[2] *Contra Apionem* ('Against Apion') 2, 1f.

Lord himself who announces what Luke's narratives will subsequently present, the events which follow take on a quite different dignity: they are presented as the realisation of sacred history.

But before we study the words of the risen Jesus, let us note—in view of our concerns in this book—only one thing about the prologue: the simple fact of the adoption of these particular stylistic means can be considered as a form of literary inculturation. Like Philo and Josephus, Luke begins by presenting his material in a form which met the expectations of an educated Greek and Roman public. The specific signals he sends evoked a sense of recognition: the reader knew (or thought he knew) what kind of book he was about to study. At the same time, Luke encodes the expectations he has of his reader in the figure of Theophilus. He may indeed have been an historical personage, but above and beyond this, he embodies for Luke the role of the ideal reader, especially thanks to his eloquent name: Theophilus means 'the friend of God', 'the one who loves God', or simply 'dear to God'. The readers Luke desires are those pious Gentile worshippers of God who may already have experienced the attractiveness of the Jewish faith in God. This gives his work an abiding relevance: 'Thus whoever is a lover of God may assume that this book is addressed to him' (the Venerable Bede). The missionary appeal is displayed here in the reserved form which is one of the characteristics of Luke's narrative theology, a form which he realises with great literary skill.

b. Two commissions

The first commission imparted by the risen Jesus to the disciples in Acts 1:4f. is that to begin with, they are to remain in Jerusalem and await the 'promise of the Father', i.e. baptism in the Spirit. This indicates an important bracketing: not only a hinge at this specific point to link the Gospel and Acts, but something that is continuously present from Lk 1 (Zechariah in the temple) until the final chapter of Acts, even if only on the horizon—namely, the city of Jerusalem, which serves as the scene from which the spreading of the Christian faith begins and as the point of reference to which it always remains related. The link between the missionary activity after Easter and the Jesus movement in the province of Galilee before Easter is established by means of Jerusalem. We might say that Jerusalem functions in Luke's two-volume work both as a real geographical symbol and as a guarantee that Christianity preserves identity with its origins.[3] Besides this, Luke employs two forms of the name of the city. He uses the indeclinable word 'Jerusalem', which is to

---

[3] Detailed arguments in support of this can be found in H.-J. Klauck, 'Die heilige Stadt. Jerusalem bei Philo und Lukas', in, *Gemeinde—Amt—Sakrament. Neutestamentliche Perspektiven,* Würzburg 1989, 101–29.

be considered as biblical Greek and more strongly evokes the Old Testament Jewish horizon; he also employs a Greek version of this, the declinable noun *Hierosolyma*, which would suggest to a Greek reader the word hieron, i.e. the temple at the heart of the city, and perhaps even the name of Solomon, the builder of that temple. (Such a deduction is etymologically incorrect, but linguistically understandable.) The biblical city, where the sanctuary founded by Solomon was the building that dominated everything else—it is hard to see how a greater amount of indirect information could be packed into a simple variation of nomenclature.

A second commission follows in the form of a promise, at Acts 1:8: '. . . and you shall be my witnesses in Jerusalem and in all Judaea and Samaria and to the end of the earth.' Most commentators correctly see this as a programmatic statement concerning the Acts of the Apostles as a whole. While not a few scholars also incline to see this as indicating the structure of the entire book, this holds good only of the initial chapters, which (as we have just mentioned) are centred on Jerusalem. In ch. 8, the 'catchment area' is extended to Samaria, coastal towns on the coastal plain follow, and a summary notice inserted at 9:31 states that 'the church throughout all Judea and Galilee and Samaria had peace . . .'—but the 'ends of the earth' are more problematic. The narrative does indeed take us later to Syria, Asia Minor and Greece, but we do not encounter genuine boundary territories like Ethiopia in the south or Spain in the west. Instead of this, Acts ends in ch. 28 with Paul's residence in the capital city, Rome. The explanation that Rome represents the entire world empire, together with its border territories, is a desperate last resort that fails to convince. It is not in the least necessary for all the predictions and announcements made in a narrative work to be fulfilled within the narrative itself; on the contrary, the tension can be increased when some of these are realised only in the period contemporary with the readers, or even point beyond this to a later date. The affirmation of the two heavenly messengers after the ascension (Acts 1:11) that Jesus will return from heaven in the same way as he went thither, transcends not only the narrative framework of Acts but also the period contemporary with its readers, since it looks ahead to the parousia at the end of time. One may certainly understand the commission to bear the gospel to the boundaries of the world—a comparable passage is Mk 13:10, 'The gospel must first be preached to all nations'—as an appeal to the readers to take their share in this task, which has not yet been completely realised. Besides this, we have just heard that Ethiopia is a boundary territory of this kind: it is natural to wonder what role the Ethiopian chamberlain (Acts 8:26–40) might play in this context, and we shall return to this point. Finally, it is impossible not to hear echoes of Is 49:6, which says of the Servant of the Lord: 'I will give you as a light to the nations, that my salvation may reach to the end of the earth', especially since Paul quotes these words in the synagogue in Pisidian Antioch and interprets them as referring to his own self (13:47). At this point in Acts 1, we lack at least one witness who is needed to carry the message further; he will be recruited only in ch. 9.

c. Jesus' departure

Luke also achieves a considerable work of interpretation and integration with the account he now gives of the ascension of Jesus (Acts 1:9–11). The Old Testament provides a prominent model of the rapture of a living person, which spares him from dying so that he stands ready to return in the final times: Elijah journeys to heaven in a fiery chariot before the eyes of his disciple Elisha (2 Kgs 2:11f.; cf. Mal 3:26f.). In terms of the history of religion, such raptures are a commonplace in the classical period. The Roman author Livy (59 BCE – 17 CE) relates a comparable story about Romulus, the legendary founder of Rome:

> After these immortal deeds, when he assembled his forces on the Field of Mars by the 'goat marsh' in order to inspect his troops, a storm suddenly broke out with loud crashes of thunder, concealing the king in such a thick shower of rain that those who were assembled could no longer see him; and after this, Romulus was no longer on earth. At length, when daylight returned, serene and calm after this tempest, the terror subsided. The men of Rome saw that the king's place was empty. Although they fully believed those senators who had stood at his side and testified that the storm had snatched him off, they were for a time speechless for sorrow, as if paralysed by the fear that they were now orphaned. A few began to hail Romulus as a god, begotten of a god, as king and father of the city of Rome, and all took up this greeting. They besought his assistance, asking him ever to watch over his people with gracious love.[4]

This model does not indeed fit Jesus perfectly, since he lived, died, was raised and appeared to his disciples. Only then was he caught up, and now he is ready to return. But the very fact that the narratives of rapture contain no exact parallels to this makes it clear what Luke intends here. He has as it were drawn on the model of rapture to lend visual form to the belief of the first Christians that Jesus was exalted to the right hand of God (Phil 2:9), illustrating this autonomous form of the Easter kerygma. He is guided here by an interest which he shares with Paul (cf. 1 Cor 15:8), viz. the desire to indicate a temporal conclusion to the Easter apparitions. The form in which he does this makes sense when seen against both the biblical-Jewish horizon and the horizon of non-Jewish Roman readers.

---

[4] *Ab urbe condita* ('From the Founding of the City Onwards') 1.16, 1–3. This text is followed by accounts of alleged apparitions of Romulus from heaven, but the evaluation of this event also contains expressions of rationalistic scepticism.

d. The kernel of the first community

Let us underline one final point. After the ascension, the kernel of the first Jerusalem community is formed in Acts 1:13f. from members of the pre-Easter Jesus movement: the eleven (without Judas), the women who had accompanied Jesus (and not, as one manuscript suggests, the wives of the apostles), Mary his mother, and his brothers. On another level, the circle of the twelve—completed only this once by the subsequent election of Matthias (1:15–26), but not after the execution of James (12:1f.)—performs a function similar to that of the city of Jerusalem. The twelve are the bearers of personal continuity, guaranteeing and handing on to future generations everything that had happened from the baptism of Jesus until his apparitions after Easter. In this special function, they are irreplaceable, whereas the group of witnesses needed for the worldwide missionary proclamation proves capable of extension: in metaphorical terms, the new family of God soon acquires further 'sisters' and 'brothers'.

2. *The Pentecost event and its consequences (Acts 2:1–47)*

a. Speaking in (foreign) tongues

The activity of proclamation cannot yet begin, because something is still lacking, namely the vitalising, inspiring power of the Spirit of God, who descends at Pentecost on all who belong to the kernel of the first community. Luke most likely employs for the specific Pentecost narrative (2:1–4) a tradition dealing with the occurrence of Spirit-inspired glossolalia, accompanied by spectacular phenomena (cf. 1 Cor 14:1–25), in the early post-Easter community.[5] We see that Luke was familiar with this glossolalia, considering it an ecstatic phenomenon linked to the Spirit, from its mention in Acts 10:44–46 (the Holy Spirit falls in the house of Cornelius on all who listen to Peter, and his companions 'hear them speaking in tongues and extolling God') and 19:2 (Paul lays hands on the disciples of John, the Holy Spirit comes upon them, and 'they speak with tongues and prophesy'). Luke shows a skill deserving the name of 'genius' when he inserts the adjective 'other' and thereby turns this 'speaking in tongues' into 'speaking in other tongues'—i.e. a miracle of speaking in foreign languages. The representatives of numerous peoples attest (in 2:6–11) that this miracle can be perceived by others: from their own standpoint, they hear the proclamation of the disciples in their own 'language' (vv. 6 and 8) or in their 'tongues' (v. 11; one should refrain from positing here a specific miracle of hearing). Luke's intention

---

[5] See now H.-J. Klauck, 'Von Kassandra bis zur Gnosis. Zum Umfeld der frühchristlichen Glossolalie', *ThQ* 179 (1999), 289–312.

here is missionary. All linguistic barriers are overthrown, making possible an unhindered communication which serves the proclamation of the gospel; the linguistic confusion that has plagued humanity since Babel is ended in a marvellous way.

Besides this, Luke has dated this event to the Feast of Weeks, the second of the great pilgrimage feasts of the Jewish year, which was celebrated as a thanksgiving for the wheat harvest (Ex 23:16). This took place seven full weeks (or fifty days) after the Passover feast, reckoned from the first day after the sabbath of the Passover week (Lev 23:15f.). It is probable that it took on a new content, as a recollection of the making of the covenant on Sinai, only after 70 CE; it is not possible to say with absolute certainty whether Luke was already familiar with this praxis. At any rate, the elaboration of what is heard and seen at Acts 2:2f., with the mighty roaring from heaven and the tongues of fire, contains theophanic motifs which accompany God's descent upon Mount Sinai in the Old Testament (cf. Ex 19:16–19: thunder and lightning crash, a heavy cloud lies upon the mountain, the sound of a mighty trumpet is heard, the Lord descends in fire, the mountain shudders; with the last element we may compare the 'renewal of Pentecost' in Acts 4:31). The manner in which Philo of Alexandria describes the transmission of the ten commandments on Mount Sinai is surely also suggestive:

> He [God] commanded that an invisible sound should be formed in the air . . . and, bestowing form on the air and changing it to a fire-red flame, should give forth a sound like a breath of air . . . Then a voice resounded from the heart of the fire that descended from heaven, filling all present with a reverent tremor, as the flame transformed itself into articulate sounds that were familiar to the hearers . . .'[6]

We need note only in passing that, according to Philo, God does not speak to human beings with his own voice (since that would be too anthropomorphic an idea of God), but instead creates a sound in the air which transforms itself into language. It is more important to observe that the sounds that people heard were familiar to them: Philo wishes to indicate here that all human beings can understand the words of the Law, if they wish. A later rabbinic legend about Sinai takes a similar line: God's voice was divided into seventy different languages for the seventy peoples of the world (cf. Gen 10:1–31), so that each people was able to hear the Law in its own tongue. This means that there are striking points of contact between Sinai and a miracle of foreign tongues—something that was certainly useful for Luke's purposes.

---

[6] *De decalogo* ('On the Ten Commandments') 33 and 46.

b. Pious Jews from the diaspora

We must note very carefully the description of the crowd, which reacts (in Acts 2:5–13) first to the roaring from heaven and then to the disciples as they speak in foreign languages. They exhibit a double reaction, initially more open and positive with the question: 'What does this mean?' in v. 12, then in tones of unambiguous rejection in v. 13: 'They are filled with new wine'—something that in fact better suits the strange glossolalia (cf. 1 Cor 14:23). It is not so appropriate to the act of speaking a foreign language perfectly, since this normally demands a clear head. The list of peoples in vv. 8–11, which we shall study in greater detail, gives the impression that these are genuinely the representatives of all lands and peoples under heaven (v. 5). But it must be pointed out that—contrary to the exaggerated indication in v. 5—this list is far from including all the lands known at that period, and also that v. 5 states that these men were pious Jews who did indeed come from the various peoples but now (without any exception) were resident in Jerusalem. Verse 11 adds to these the proselytes who had converted to Judaism.

These Jews from the diaspora are not staying for a short period in Jerusalem, for example as pilgrims to the festival: this is where they live. Social history permits us to confirm what is stated here. In the classical period, just as in modern times, there were many Jews in the whole world who yearned to settle in the city of Jerusalem when they were older, after having acquired a modest prosperity in foreign parts. This state of affairs is attested in the Acts of the Apostles by the existence in Jerusalem of synagogue communities from Cyrene, Alexandria, Cilicia and Asia Minor (6:9), or by the presence of a man such as Barnabas, born in Cyprus (4:36).

In this passage, Luke has several other compositional goals, and he succeeds in realising them simultaneously. According to the 'plot' of Acts, it would still have been much too early for a direct mission to the Gentiles. By designating the witnesses to the Pentecost events 'as *Jews*, Luke avoids the premature notion of the Gentile mission; and by describing them as *diaspora Jews* who have taken up permanent residence in Jerusalem, he avoids the difficulty of having them return to their own countries as baptised persons who could proclaim the gospel there—for that, once again, would be premature.'[7] But at the same time, they do represent their own countries of origin, as well as the native populations there with their own local dialects. Otherwise, Hebrew or Aramaic would have been enough for communication in Jerusalem, with at most Latin and Greek providing supplementary help. Thus we have a miniature preliminary model of the future opening up to the entire world.

---

[7] A. Weiser, *Apg*, 87.

c. The list of peoples

The list of peoples in vv. 8–11 serves the purpose of affirming this. It is remarkable (even if in fact seldom noticed) that this list is offered in direct speech. This means that it is presented as something recited in unison by the numerous crowd, an achievement surely hardly less deserving of admiration than the disciples' speaking in foreign languages. In its present form,[8] it contains seventeen *membra*, but one can consider the 'Jews and proselytes' at the end of v. 10 as a redactional insertion by Luke, with the intention of clarifying v. 5. The same is true of the 'visitors from Rome' in the same verse, in view of the goal of Acts as a whole.

This leaves us with fourteen *membra*; we need not discuss here whether this number can be reduced still further by the elimination of the 'Cretans and Arabians' (as dwellers on islands and in deserts) or the 'Judaeans' in v. 9. The possibility of arriving at the number twelve for the original list is indeed tempting, especially since this might suggest a model in astrological texts which assign twelve countries to the twelve signs of the zodiac. But we need not go as far as this. Lists of peoples are also found in the geographers and (more relevant to us) the historians. For example, Curtius Rufus summarises the conquests of Alexander the Great in the following list, which has fourteen (!) *membra*: 'Caria, Lydia, Cappadocia, Phrygia, Paphlagonia, Pamphylia, Pisidia, Cilicia, Syria, Phoenicia, Armenia, Persia, Media and Parthia are subject to our power.'[9] Philo gives a list of all the regions in which (as far as he knows) Jews are to be found, taking the opportunity to interpret in very generous terms the marginalised existence of diaspora Judaism, which was far from universally welcome, as a conscious politics of colonialisation conducted from the metropolis, Jerusalem:

> She [i.e. the city of Jerusalem] is the metropolis not only of one country, namely Judea, but also of most other countries, thanks to the colonies which she has established over the course of time in neighbouring lands, in Egypt, the greater part of Asia Minor as far as Bithynia and the hinterlands of Pontus, as well as in Europe, Thessaly, Boeotia, Macedonia, Aetolia, Attica, Argos, Corinth and in most of the regions of the Peloponnese, specifically in its most significant regions. Not only are the mainlands full of Jewish settlements, but also the most celebrated islands: Euboea, Cyprus and Crete . . .[10]

Unlike Philo, Luke does not include Greece in his list of peoples. Rome was probably not found in the pre-Lukan tradition, and this means that the west as a whole was missing. If we check where the various countries

---

[8] Cf. W. Stenger, 'Beobachtungen zur sogenannten Völkerliste des Pfingstwunders (*Apg* 2, 7–11)', *Kairos* 21 (1979), 206–14.

[9] *The history of Alexander* 6.3, 3.

[10] *Legatio ad Gaium* ('Embassy to Caligula') 281f.

are to be found on a map, we observe that they are all located in the eastern half of the Mediterranean world and that the list moves in an S-shape from north-east (Black Sea) to south-west (North Africa); in this context, it is particularly noteworthy that Syria is missing. The catalogue reflects earlier political circumstances that obtained before the Romans took power, in the period of the successor kings to Alexander the Great, circumstances also reflected in the quotation from Curtius Rufus above. It is possible that Luke employed an earlier text which listed synagogue communities in the successor kingdoms to Alexander from the perspective of the Jewish community in the Syrian capital, Antioch; this would explain why Syria itself is missing from the list. But since source materials are lacking, this remains only a hypothesis—though an attractive one.

One can however make the following point. In the narratives about Alexander, such lists were designed to provide an overview of conquered territories. In Luke's work, a new world-view is just beginning to conquer a world empire, not with a mighty army and the force of weapons, but only by means of itinerant messengers of the gospel and by the might inherent in the word they proclaim. Thus the Christian reception of the genre 'lists of peoples' resembles in many ways the Jewish reception, for although Philo can speak of conquered territories, he does not really succeed in hiding the fact that his people leads a wretched existence in the diaspora as a persecuted and oppressed minority. Nevertheless, neither movement can be 'liquidated', since their vitality is too strong.

d. The quotation from Joel

Peter's sermon at Pentecost begins at Acts 2:16–21 with a long quotation from Joel 2:28–32 (or 3:1–5 in the Septuagint), which also has great programmatic significance for all that follows.[11] Apart from the pro-phetical interpretation of the outpouring of the Spirit as a sign of the final ages, the inclusive traits are especially noteworthy: sons and daughters will prophesy, young men and old will have visionary dreams, the Spirit will descend upon male and female servants. We can make the point in more abstract terms by saying that men and women, old and young, free and slave are addressed. It is only the final pair from Gal 3:28, Jews and Gentiles, that we do not find here.

At this point, Luke encounters a problem, since the promise in Joel is made in fact only to those of Israel who return home, and it is linked exclusively to Jerusalem. Indeed, there follows in Joel 4 a punitive judge-ment over all the Gentile nations, who are handed over to destruction.

---

[11] For details, cf. H. van de Sandt, 'The Fate of the Gentiles in Joel and Acts 2. An Intertextual Study', *EthL* 66 (1990), 56–77; G. J. Steyn, *Septuagint Quotations in the Context of the Petrine and Pauline Speeches of the Acta Apostolorum* (Contributions to Biblical Exegesis and Theology 12), Kampen 1995, 69–100.

Accordingly, Luke breaks off the quotation in good time, refraining from employing the conclusion of Joel 2:32 (or 3:5), although he could have used this, at least in the Septuagint version: 'and the preachers of the good news, whom the Lord calls'. In Luke's narrative, the gathering on Mount Zion and the outpouring of the Spirit promised in Joel have just happened (Acts 1–2), so that this need not be repeated as such. The Christian message is freed from every exclusive geographical restriction, so that it can set out on its path into the world. Luke effects the inclusion of the Gentiles—something not found in Joel—by means of an allusion to Is 57:19: 'For the promise is to you and to your children and to all that are far off, everyone whom the Lord our God calls to him' (Acts 2:39). Those 'far off' might indeed be other diaspora Jews, who (unlike those mentioned in Acts 2:5) are still resident aliens in their respective countries, but it is probable that the non-Jewish inhabitants can be seen standing, scarcely concealed, behind them (cf. Eph 2:17).

As a direct consequence of Peter's sermon, the community increases by roughly three thousand new members (Acts 2:41); if things had continued at this tempo, Jerusalem would sooner or later have been transformed into a wholly Christian city. But this information about growth (cf. also 2:47) also points ahead to the strengthening of the communities in the non-Jewish world. The first of several lengthy summaries appears in Acts 2:42–47, describing the conditions of the ideal community life, with property held in common, the celebration of meals and prayers in abiding harmony. These golden pictures from the life of the earliest community explain the attractiveness of the new group, which for the first time realises, in exemplary fashion, the long-desired social utopias of the classical world. The future basis of missionary activity also appears in Acts 2:46, with the mention of the houses in which bread is broken.[12]

---

[12] For more detail on the summaries, the fellowship of property and the house, see H.-J. Klauck, 'Die Hausgemeinde als Lebensform im Urchristentum', 'Gütergemeinschaft in der klassischen Antike, in Qumran und im Neuen Testament', 'Die Armut der Jünger aus der Sicht des Lukas', in *Gemeinde—Amt—Sakrament* (see n. 3 above), 11–28, 69–100, 160–94.

II

THE EVANGELIST PHILIP (ACTS 8)

We pass here over the accounts in the following chapters of the developments and conflicts in Jerusalem, noting only that Luke lists the names of the group of seven 'deacons' around Stephen at Acts 6:5. Historically speaking, these can be identified as the body of leaders of the hellenistic, Greek-speaking part of the first community in Jerusalem. It is not by chance that the second name Luke mentions, directly after Stephen, is that of Philip,[1] who must be distinguished from the apostle with the same name, one of the twelve (cf. 1:13). We encounter this Philip as an evangelist, i.e. one who proclaims the good news, at 21:8f., when Paul stays at the house of Philip in Caesarea on his journey to Jerusalem, and we also learn in this passage that he has four daughters with prophetic gifts. He is the central figure in the two scenes in Acts 8, first in Samaria and then on the road from Jerusalem to Gaza.

1. *In Samaria (Acts 8:4–25)*

In the wake of the martyrdom of Stephen, a persecution assailed the community in Jerusalem, so that many of its members had to leave the city (8:1). This seemed to pose a grave risk to the very existence of the infant Christian group, but God's providential governance turned it into a blessing: those who were driven out made use of the opportunity to proclaim the gospel in a decisive manner in the regions in which they found themselves (8:4). The hostile actions unleashed a fruitful impulse with a dynamism that went as far as Syrian Antioch (11:19). This warded off the danger of stagnation which might otherwise have come. Besides this, the time is close at hand for the fulfilment of the next stage in the programmatic sketch of the earliest Christian missionary movement at 1:8: 'You shall be my witnesses in Jerusalem and in all Judea and *Samaria . . .*'.

Thus the evangelist Philip arrives at 8:5 in a city (or, according to a textual variant, in *the* city) of Samaria. It is difficult to identify this city. It may be—especially if we accept the reading 'the city'—that the capital,

---

[1] For a detailed study of his person, of the relevant texts and secondary literature, see: F. S. Spencer, *The Portrait of Philip in Acts. A Study of Roles and Relations* (JSNT.S 67), Sheffield 1992; and now the excellent monograph by A. von Dobbeler, *Der Evangelist Philippus in der Geschichte des Urchristentums. Eine prosopographische Studie* (TANZ 30), Tübingen and Basle 2000, esp. 37–215 (on Acts 8).

Samaria, is meant. Herod the Great had changed its name to 'Sebaste' (the Greek for 'Augustus') in honour of the emperor Augustus, and had equipped it with a temple for the imperial cult. Another possibility is Shechem, the ancient religious centre. Its modern name, Nablus, is derived from the new name of 'Neapolis' which Titus bestowed on it after 72 CE.

The territory of Samaria, lying to the north of Jerusalem between Judaea and Galilee, has a history all of its own. Its original inhabitants, the Samaritans, can be considered as half-siblings or hostile brothers of the Jewish people. After a split which can be dated roughly to the fifth century before the Common Era, they retained the Pentateuch as their sacred scripture and continued to celebrate the Passover feast according to the old rite, but they had their own temple on Mount Gerizim, refusing to acknowledge the temple in Jerusalem. Strictly speaking, one should distinguish this group from those 'Samaritans' who were non-Jewish, pagan inhabitants of this area. It is understandable that the latter tended above all to cluster in a city like Sebaste, which by now was hellenised or Romanised. But it is questionable whether Luke, who also displays a striking interest in the Samaritans in the texts specific to his own Gospel (cf. the inhospitable Samaritans at Lk 9:51–56; the compassionate Samaritan at 10:25–37; the grateful Samaritan at 17:11–19), is at all interested in such a distinction. In his eyes, Samaria was a welcome transition zone, geographically and religiously speaking, from Judaism to paganism. Thus the twilight vagueness, which lies over the information he provides and makes it difficult to define from the perspective of the history of religions what he is telling us, is a direct advantage from his own point of view.

What Philip does in this city is a replica of what Jesus did in Galilee before Easter: he proclaims the good news of the lordship of God (Acts 8:12), now expanded to include the name of Jesus Christ (8:5), and he performs miraculous deeds, more specifically healings and exorcisms. It is obvious that those healed would react with great joy (8:8); but the conversion of numerous men and women and their baptism is somewhat detached from the mention of the miraculous signs and is linked at 8:12 primarily to the words of Philip's preaching.

a. Simon 'Magus'

A narrative flashback at Acts 8:9–11 introduces a new person named Simon, an inhabitant of the city and presumably a Samaritan. Luke tells us twice, at v. 9 and v. 11, that he had practised magic and had literally driven the populace to ecstasy with his magical tricks.[2] He himself asserts

---

[2] On Simon and the manner in which Luke portrays him, see F. Heintz, *Simon 'le magicien'. Actes 8,5–23 et l'accusation de magie contre les prophètes thaumaturges dans l'Antiquité* (CRB 39), Paris 1997.

that he is 'somebody great' (v. 9), and the meaning of this claim becomes clearer when we hear the people profess their conviction in the form of an acclamation: 'This man is that power of God which is called Great' (v. 10).

Here we must first reflect on the significance of the accusation of magic, and on what is really meant by this remarkable acclamation, which appears to accord with Simon's own self-understanding. 'The great power' is a designation which, taken in isolation, can serve as a euphemism for the divine name itself, e.g. in Samaritan sources and in magical texts. Nevertheless, its use does not necessarily imply an identification of the human being Simon with God or (putting it more cautiously) with a god; all that need be indicated is a 'divine human being', to use a somewhat imprecise though serviceable category drawn from the study of the history of religions. The predicate 'divine', or even 'god', is bestowed on prominent individuals, mostly wonder-workers, doctors, philosophers, rulers and kings, since these were seen as immediate bearers and mediators of divine powers. The Pre-Socratic philosopher Empedocles goes very far in this direction, when he affirms:

> I travel around as an immortal god, no longer mortal, acclaimed with honours by all, as is fitting in my case . . . Some people demand prophecies from me, others ask for information about sicknesses of all kinds, looking to hear a word that will bring healing, since they have long been tormented by piercing pains.[3]

No doubt, these are very resonant words which go beyond what Acts says about Simon here. But if we simply consider this phenomenon objectively, it is not so far removed from what we could call the 'representation of Christ' by the Christian messengers, if we recall such logia as Lk 10:16, 'Whoever hears you, hears me.' It is obvious that Christian missionaries could not simply remain inactive when they encountered representatives of this type of 'divine human being'. It was necessary to draw boundary lines and indicate the differences, even if this meant blackening the reputation of one's opponents.

This is the framework within which we must see the accusation of practising magic in some specific manner. The classical period was familiar with two kinds of magic, which one may call black and white magic. The Greek language adopted the term 'magician' as a loan-word from Persian, where it denoted a highly respected, learned and wise member of a priestly caste. Even the New Testament permits us to sense something of this, when 'magicians from the rising of the sun', wise men from the East, come looking for the new-born Jesus (Mt 2:1). The other, negative significance of this word, with which we are familiar, did

---

[3] Fragments of the Pre-Socratics (Diels-Kranz), 31 B 112.

indeed become dominant in the course of time; but Philo can still draw a comparison between the two uses:

> It is not only private persons, but kings too—even the greatest among them— who practise genuine magic, which is a science of seeing that employs clearer ideas to illuminate the works of nature and deserves veneration and respect. This applies especially to the kings of the Persians, so that among them no one can attain the royal dignity unless he has previously had close contact with the magicians. But magic is a distortion of this art—to put it correctly, a real perversion of it—when it is carried out by itinerant beggars, mountebanks, women of the most disreputable sort and slaves, who promise to effect a purification or atonement by magical means and to use love-potions and secret spells to induce deadly hatred in lovers and most passionate love in those who hate, leading astray and luring those above all who are simple and harmless . . .[4]

So who was this Simon, who is always designated by the surname Magus, which we owe to Luke? A number of factors make it difficult to answer this question. In the second century, there existed gnostic groups which called themselves Simonians and asserted that Simon Magus was their founder. The church fathers who attacked heresies took this up and made Simon Magus not only the founder of the Simonians, but of gnosis as a whole. For example, Irenaeus of Lyons writes about him, *c.*180 CE:

> First, there is Simon from Samaria, the well-known magician . . . He pretended to be a believer, since he thought that the apostles performed their healings by means of magic, rather than by the power of God . . . It is said that the emperor Claudius, during whose reign he lived, honoured him for his magical arts with a statue. He was venerated by many people like a god. He taught that it was he who had appeared to the Jews as the Son, had descended in Samaria as the Father, and had come to the other peoples as the Holy Spirit, and that he was the most exalted power, i.e. the one who is above everything, as Father . . . [His disciples] too possess an image of Simon, based on the figure of Zeus, and one of Helena based on the figure of Minerva, and they worship these images. They also possess a name: after the inventor of their despicable teaching, they call themselves Simonians. It is with them that the so-called gnosis began . . .[5]

Some scholars in modern times have agreed with this position, and it has its proponents even today, since it seems to open up a possibility of tracing a lineage back via the disciples and followers of Simon: the beginning of gnosis could thus be dated to this early period, *c.*30–40 CE (otherwise, our earliest source materials derive from the second century).

---

[4] Philo, *De specialibus legibus* ('On the Individual Laws') 3, 100f.
[5] Irenaeus, *Adversus haereses* ('Against the Heresies') 1.23, 1–4.

But this hypothesis merits little confidence. The gnostics searched the Bible to find male and female ancestors, and their attitude of protest led them consciously to choose prominent negative figures like Cain, Judas and Simon Magus; the church fathers took this fiction at face value. Thus we need not suppose—as would inevitably be the case, if the gnostic hypothesis were correct—that Luke's polemic has downgraded the head of a significant gnostic school to a mere magician.

Recently, the opposite path has been taken, with the suggestion that Simon was the founder of an autonomous Samaritan Christianity which the first community in Jerusalem did not accept and integrate (as it did with Pauline Christianity); Luke's distorted description would be an expression of this lack of consensus.[6] But the best option is surely to leave the picture of Simon as open as possible. We should also note that the apologist Justin, who himself came from Shechem, writes, c.160 CE, of Simon Magus as an historical person, saying that he was born in Gitta in Samaria. This Simon discovered a situation of religious need in his native land which allowed him to work successfully as a performer of miracles, a soothsayer and a counsellor in all the different circumstances of people's lives. His prominent position makes it historically plausible that he came into conflict with those who proclaimed the Christian message. Luke skilfully employs the suspicion of magic to cope with this situation of competition. When systems competed against each other, this accusation regularly provided a handy instrument: one party would accuse the other of black magic, hurling its entire available arsenal of abuse and polemics. As for one's own group, it practised at most magic of the older, unreservedly positive kind—unless one preferred *a priori* to avoid the risk of even the remotest connection between one's own side and the concept of magic.

b. Simon and Philip

Acts 8:13 relates the outcome of the encounter in Samaria between Philip, the new arrival, and Simon, who had already been active there for some time. This verse is probably a redactional formulation by Luke, intended to weld various traditions together. One would expect a contest between the two, but in our text Simon admits defeat all along the line, before any contest actually breaks out. He acknowledges Philip's superiority and hence comes to faith and accepts baptism (we should note that Luke is the only source to tell us that Simon became a Christian). From now on, Simon keeps close to Philip. As v. 13 emphasises, he was impressed

[6] See K. Berger, 'Propaganda und Gegenpropaganda im frühen Christentum: Simon Magus als Gestalt des samaritanischen Christentums', in *Religious Propaganda and Missionary Competition in the New Testament World* (Festschrift for D. Georgi) (NT.S 74), Leiden 1994, 313–17.

above all by the signs and wonders worked by Philip. This is in accord with his own earlier activity as worker of miracles—he knows good professional work when he sees it. But the fact that here (unlike in v. 12) Philip's proclamation of the work is not mentioned as a motivation for faith, brings us one step closer to the solution of the puzzle.

This is because the reasons that led Simon to be baptised remain a matter of dispute. Like other church fathers, Irenaeus assessed these as impure. In the text quoted above, he says that Simon's conversion was nothing more than an act of hypocrisy. All that Simon wanted was to uncover the mystery he assumed to lie behind the miraculous power of the Christian missionaries; this would be the reason for his devotion to Philip. This type of explanation runs all through the history of interpretation, even into modern commentaries, but it imports into v. 13 from vv. 18f. the problem of Simon's renewed bad behaviour. If, instead of this, one looks at v. 13 on the basis of what precedes it, another interpretation is possible: Simon's conversion and faith are indeed generated by a subjectively honest attitude, but his faith is not yet so firm as it ought to be. Simon's previous activities have left their mark on him in the form of a deficit: he bases his faith too exclusively on miracles, too little on the word. Much remains to be done, before he can overcome this one-sidedness, and the constant company of Philip would give Simon the opportunity for this. His precarious faith has the potential to become stable, but for the moment it remains at risk. If one interprets the text otherwise, one would have to cast doubt on the human qualities of the Philip who falls for such a transparent trick.

Our final reflection on Acts 8:5–13 concerns the striking 'mirrorings' outlined in this pericope, i.e. the fact that a number of affirmations are made twice. The people 'all gave heed' to the words of Philip (v. 6), but previously they had already 'given heed' to Simon and his deeds (vv. 8f.). Simon is described as the 'great power' (v. 10), while we are told of Philip's 'great deeds of power' (v. 13): these miraculous signs form the contrast to Simon's magic. While the people first rejoiced about Philip and were astounded at Simon, this happens to Simon himself in v. 13; and like the crowd in v. 12, he too comes to faith in v. 13 and accepts baptism. Literary skill is employed surreptitiously to relate Philip and Simon Magus to one another in such a way that what emerges in the final analysis is Philip's superiority and the otherness of what he is doing. Why, however, must these two points be emphasised with such vigour? It is because an objective consideration will note a suspicious similarity between the public appearance and working of Philip and of Simon; it is to some extent a question of interpretation, whether a successful healing is attributed to a miracle or to sorcery. These 'mirrorings' show that the experiential world in which the author and his readers lived was aware that most religious phenomena were ambiguous and required interpretation. Without interpretation, the phenomena have no value; this is what makes it so difficult to distinguish the working of miracles from magical activity.

Our text shows us one further reason why the system of values which Philip represents proves superior: whereas Simon proclaims himself when he says that he is someone great, Philip proclaims someone else, namely Jesus Christ. From the perspective of the Christian narrator, Simon performs his miracles on the basis of his claim to embody in his own person a divine power present among human beings, while Philip keeps the necessary distance between his own self and the God and Lord in whose commission he works. He is inspired by the Spirit, a power that is not his own property but is bestowed in each individual instance as God's free gift. Only the Spirit performs true miracles. This construction may ultimately remain fragile, when one submits it to critical analysis, but it does at any rate indicate an awareness of the existing problems and an attempt to draw up a list of criteria to deal with them.

c. The reception of the Spirit

Philip now leaves the narrative, to reappear only in the following scene (Acts 8:26–40). The senior apostles in Jerusalem hear of the fine missionary success in Samaria, and send Peter and John there. Through their prayer and the laying on of their hands, the newly baptised Samaritans receive the Holy Spirit (8:14–17). Questions at once arise. Was Philip not capable of this? Is the bestowal of the Holy Spirit reserved to the bearers of a higher office? More importantly still, do not baptism and the reception of the Spirit belong inseparably together in earliest Christian thought; does not each one receive in his heart the 'down-payment' of the Spirit at baptism? The difficulty is increased by the fact that Luke knows of other arrangements too. As we shall see, the reception of the Spirit precedes the act of baptism at Acts 10:44–48. At 1:5, on the feast of Pentecost, the pure experience of the Spirit is described meta-phorically as baptism. At 9:17f., Ananias, a Christian in Damascus but certainly not an apostle, lays his hands on Saul, who is thereupon filled by the Spirit and accepts baptism. If we look somewhat further afield, we see that Paul himself interprets baptism at 1 Cor 12:13 as an incorporation into the community, brought about by the Spirit. Is there an utter disorder at work here?

We glimpse the outlines of a solution when we differentiate between various elements in the event of baptism—the forgiveness of sins, the bestowal of the gift of the Spirit, admission into the community—and when we reflect that the Spirit's working is not linked exclusively to baptism. As is well known, he blows where he wills. In terms of the content of the symbols employed, baptism with water, considered on its own, evokes more strongly the washing away of sins and hence individual conversion. The bestowal of the Spirit, which is linked to the laying on of hands, tends more towards the establishing of community and church. The various elements can come together in one single action, but they can also be separated, making it possible to reflect on each one individually. Luke deconstructs the unified process into its individual elements and varies their arrangement according to context. Here (to use an abstract theological concept), he is interested in the unity of the Church. He separates baptism and the reception of the Spirit temporally in order to link the new foundation in Samaria to Jerusalem. The city is the geographical turning-point, and he also introduces representatives of the Twelve as guarantors of personal continuity. The Samaritans experience their own feast of Pentecost, which aligns them as a young Church with the Pentecostal community in Jerusalem, in terms of salvation history. The unspectacular quality of the event in Samaria—without a mighty roar from heaven as at 2:2, or a moving of the place where they are as at 4:31—is no argument against this interpretation. Perhaps the phenomena which may have accompanied such events were suppressed here, in view of Simon Magus' weakness; it is also possible that their existence is simply presupposed, in analogy to the other occasions when the Spirit was bestowed.

d. Lapsing

Simon Magus, at any rate, reacts in his own way. The text makes it clear that he himself is one of those who receive, not only baptism, but also the Spirit. He draws his conclusion, with or without the help of particular phenomena. He is correct to identify the Spirit as the decisive power that inspired Philip in the miracles he performed. It would be useful to possess this Spirit in such a stable manner that one could transmit it at will to others, for example to heal them or to empower them to work miracles in their turn. Such considerations lie behind his request for this authority, and his offer to pay money for it.

If no false notes have been sounded in the story up to this point, now at any rate a shrill disharmony is introduced with this offer of cash, and not only because Simon thereby involuntarily gave his name to the later crime of simony in canon law, understood as abuses connected with the sale of spiritual things and offices.[7] The reader spontaneously asks where Simon got this money, and the answer will be that it had been amassed in the course of his previous lucrative activity as a famous magician. Like almost all his professional colleagues, he practised only for a fee. If he is now willing to invest a large sum, he does so in hope of even higher earnings in the future: this new power of the Spirit will help him to offer

---

[7] See H. O. Lüthi, art. 'Simonie', *LThK* second edn IX, 774–6, with this fine example: the sale of a consecrated chalice is not simony, 'unless the price was raised because the chalice was consecrated' (775).

a wider spectrum of services and so win new clients. Moreover, if one bears in mind Luke's well-known sensitivity in matters of money and possessions, one perceives that this step on Simon's part will end badly.

In the pre-Lukan tradition, which knew Simon only as a Samaritan miracle worker, not as a baptised Christian, these problems were not so acutely present. His confrontation with Simon Peter was indeed inevitable, but other presuppositions meant that it was less significant, and its consequences less severe. In the context of our Lukan text, we are compelled to ask how this new public backsliding is compatible with Simon's conversion (v. 13) and whether, at worst, Simon is guilty of the sin against the Holy Spirit whom he has received (cf. Lk 10:12).

We have already seen one type of solution: the information given in vv. 18f. is retrojected on to v. 13, and hypocritical intentions are attributed to Simon, whose new faith was only a façade, not seriously meant. If one refuses this solution and takes Simon's faith in v. 13 as honest (albeit precarious), vv. 18f. can be explained in at least equally plausible terms. Here, the appropriate category is that of lapsing. Painful experiences have taught Luke that some people do in fact take the decision of faith too superficially. Their past catches up with the newly-baptised; despite all their goodwill, they fail the first test of their strength. He has portrayed this metaphorically in the exposition of the parable of the sower, where we are told that some receive the word with joy, 'but these have no root: they believe for a while and in time of temptation fall away'. In the case of others, the initial faith is 'choked by the cares and riches and pleasures of life' (Lk 8:13f.). Wealth is already mentioned here as a disturbing factor, and it plays an inglorious role in two especially terrible cases, viz. Judas Iscariot, who was one of the Twelve yet betrayed Jesus for money, and Ananias and Sapphira, members of the Christian community in Jerusalem who were severely punished for their attempt to keep a part of their income secret (Acts 5:1–11). At this point in the narrative, it seems likely that Simon Magus will take his place in their ranks. The sudden prospect of quick profits has made him forget his initial enthusiasm for the new faith, so that he lapses into old patterns of behaviour.

But how does one deal with those who lapse? The following verses are meant to answer this question; but let us first emphasise that Luke employs an additional criterion of differentiation when he deals with the topic of money. Unlike the typical professional magician, the apostles and disciples of Jesus perform their miracles without payment. They demand no fee, and reject one indignantly if it is offered. Consequently, they themselves lead a poor and modest life. 'I have no silver and gold,' says Peter to the lame beggar at the temple gate before he heals him (Acts 3:6), and Paul insists on this point in his farewell discourse: 'I coveted no one's silver or gold or apparel' (20:33), in accordance with a logion of Jesus which is not transmitted in any of the Gospels: 'It is more blessed to give than to receive' (20:35). This does not, of course, mean that these sentiments were perfectly practised in real life. But even in the late Acts of Thomas, this is the one distinguishing characteristic that people observe in the case of the apostle Thomas:

> He goes around in cities and villages and gives what he has to the poor. He teaches about a new god and cares for the sick and casts out demons. He does many other miracles too. And we believe that he is a magician. But his deeds of mercy and the healings that he performs without taking any fee show that he is righteous . . .[8]

e. Simon Magus and Simon Peter

In v. 20, Peter begins to preach in prophetic tones about punishment and repentance. His sermon is full of Old Testament allusions and reminiscences. The Spirit is God's free gift and must not be devalued to an object of commercial transactions; Simon is threatened with the loss of salvation, and something like a formula of excommunication in v. 21 excludes him from the fellowship of believers. All the more surprising, then, is the appeal to a change of heart in v. 22: 'Repent therefore of this wickedness of yours, and pray to the Lord that, if possible, the intent of your heart may be forgiven you.' If one takes these words seriously, then Simon Magus has not committed the unforgiveable sin against the Holy Spirit, and Luke—unlike the Letter to the Hebrews (cf. 6:4–6; 10:26–31)—offers backsliding Christians the possibility of a renewed conversion and a second repentance.

In v. 24, Simon Magus's reaction is not at all stubborn, but rather shows insight and repentance (intensified in Codex D by the addition: 'He did not cease to shed many tears'). This can also be seen in a sensitive choice of words: at v. 22, Peter adjures Simon: 'Pray to the Lord,' and Simon picks this up at v. 24, when he says to Peter and John: 'Pray for me to the Lord, that nothing of what you have said may come upon me.' He has greater trust in the intercession of these men of God than in his own requests, though this does not mean that he himself will not pray, as Peter has charged him to do. Thus, Simon shows that all this has had an effect on him. The harsh penitential sermon has touched a nerve in him and he does not want to be banished for ever from the community of salvation.

But what will happen to Simon Magus in the future? What are his prospects? The Acts of the Apostles have nothing to say about this, whereas later Christian tradition supplies an unambiguous answer. The common understanding of v. 13 was that one whose conversion to the

---

[8] Acts of Thomas 20.

faith was motivated by sheer hypocrisy could not be capable of genuine repentance. Simon Magus is lost for ever to the Church; all he is fit for now is to be head of all heretics and founder of all heresies. The Acts of Peter elaborate the rest of his life story with especial vividness, portraying a competition in miracles between Peter and Simon Magus in Rome. Simon Magus loses, and meets a disgraceful death.

This interpretative tradition is surely not in keeping with the intention of Luke's open conclusion. Luke consciously refrains from telling us whether Simon Magus is saved or perishes, because his aim here is to make an appeal to his readers. Sadly, it often happens that believers lapse in the way described above, and then a severe call to repentance is required. What happens next, depends not least on the behaviour of the sinner himself.

We can develop this idea a little further. The specific risk to which Simon was exposed could affect other members of the Christian communities too, since the religious practices they knew before their conversion to Christianity are not forgotten and laid aside once and for all. If the circumstances are right, these can suddenly regain their attractiveness: for example, when someone is in despair and feels that prayer has ceased to help, he will take refuge again in the magic with which he is familiar. In the long term, Christian office-bearers too are at risk of making their own persons the theme of their preaching, with the intention of making financial gain; this is not merely some exotic form of the corruption and perversion of religion. Thus, Luke's polemic here is directed against the remnants of popular pagan belief in the Christian communities and against systemic risks incurred by Christian office-bearers. This is why, instead of presenting the text of a sermon, he chooses to clothe the matter in a narrative with an open conclusion which reaches into the period contemporary with the reader. Precisely this is the genius of Luke's narrative theology.

2. *On the road to Gaza (Acts 8:26–40)*

Philip, whom we had left in Samaria, comes into action again at Acts 8:26. An angel of the Lord charges him to make his way on foot to the road which goes southwest from Jerusalem to Gaza. This road is long (more than one hundred kilometres) and deserted, but as soon as Philip reaches it, he encounters a chariot rolling southwards. Now it is no longer the angel, but the Spirit who tells him to join the chariot (8:29); after the close of this episode, it is once again the Spirit who will snatch him away and transport him across a great distance to Azotus (8:39f.), so that he can work as a missionary there and in the neighbouring coastal towns until he finally reaches Caesarea, where he will once again be needed at 21:8. This miraculous transport is similar to what happens in the Old Testament to Ezekiel (Ezek 11:24, 'And the Spirit lifted me up and brought me in the vision by the Spirit of God into Chaldea, to the exiles') and Habakkuk (Dan 14:36, 'Then the angel of the Lord took him by the crown of his head, and lifted him by his hair and set him down in Babylon . . .'). We hear of speculations that the same thing might have happened to Elijah (1 Kgs 18:12; 2 Kgs 2:16, 'It may be that the Spirit of the Lord has caught him up and cast him upon some mountain or into some valley'). The fact that Philip acts twice at the (often abrupt) dictate of an angel and the Spirit identifies him as a charismatic-prophetic wandering missionary, travelling above all in the strongly hellenised, half-pagan coastal region. This immediately prompts a supposition about the *Sitz-im-Leben* of the pre-Lukan narrative unit: it was presumably transmitted in the groups of hellenistic Jewish Christians as a legend about the person of Philip, with the purpose of employing his example to justify their own decision to do missionary work among the Gentiles. This comment is not intended to question whether Philip did in fact achieve such a startling individual conversion; on the contrary, such a conversion will have generated the process of tradition.

a. The Ethiopian chamberlain

We already know Philip from Samaria, but the man who is now to be his dialogue partner is new to us. Luke's presentation at vv. 27–28 displays all his skill in the narrative description of persons. Using only a few attributes and relative clauses, he lets us see the picture of a living personality.

Of necessity, other persons had to accompany him (cf. especially v. 38: 'And he commanded the chariot to stop'), but these are omitted from the narrative. The first thing we are told about the man sitting in the chariot is that he is an *Ethiopian*. The Ethiopia of the classical period was not located on the territory of the modern Ethiopian state, but corresponds to today's northern Sudan, immediately south of Egypt. The Greek term 'Ethiopians', translated literally, means something like 'burnt face' or 'fire face', indicating that those who live there are dark-skinned. Since the regions farther south had never yet been penetrated, it was felt that Ethiopia lay at the borders of the world; it suffices here to read two lines from the beginning of Homer's *Odyssey*: Poseidon 'was with the far-off Ethiopians, the people who live *at the outermost edge*' (*Od.* 1, 21f.; cf. also Is 43:3, 6).

The next thing we are told about this man is that he is a *eunuch* (something that the official German Catholic translation hops over in silence!). Closely linked to this, he is described as a high *official*. The basic meaning of 'eunuch' designates one mutilated or castrated, deprived of his procreative faculty when young by means of a brutal surgical intervention. It was indeed possible for eunuchs to rise to high positions at the courts of princes and kings, and (for obvious reasons) especially at the courts of female rulers, but not even this protected them from discrimination and mockery: they looked like weaklings and had soft voices, so that they were the object of ridicule. Despite the operation they had undergone, they were often suspected of unbridled lust: in many cases, only the testicles were removed, and it was thought that they were still capable of sexual intercourse with women—without needing to fear that children would be the result of such acts. The satirist Lucian of Samosata is one of those who use harsh words about them. He devoted a work, *The Eunuch*, specifically to reviling them, demanding that eunuchs should be forbidden to study philosophy: indeed, 'such half-men ought to be excluded from all participation in sacred things and from all public assemblies and associations' (6). This summarises their total marginalisation: religious ('sacred things'), political ('public assemblies') and social ('associations').

In the course of time, however, 'eunuch' had also become a generic term that could be applied to court officials who were completely intact, physically speaking. The juxtaposition of 'eunuch' and 'official' in v. 27 could be explained as follows: the man was a 'eunuch' only in terms of his position, not of his physical characteristics. This question is very important for the exposition of the text because, as we shall see shortly, the answer to it defines the relationship of the Ethiopian to Judaism. In my view, the juxtaposition of the two words suggests rather that we should attach full weight to each, so that the nexus means that the man was physically mutilated and at the same time (as so often) a high official at court: first we are told something about his physical condition, then about his profession. The man is consistently called a eunuch—four times in vv. 34–39—and this evidence from within the text itself likewise suggests that we should accept the obvious, realistic meaning of the word. Ultimately, it is only this argument that counts, especially since we no longer have access to the historical details.

A further piece of information Luke gives is that the eunuch was an official of *Candace, queen of the Ethiopians*. This suggests initially that the queen of Ethiopia at that period was called 'Candace'; we might perhaps even go so far as to suppose (as in some commentaries) that Ethiopia was always ruled by queens. Neither supposition is correct. Like 'Pharaoh' in Egyptian, 'Candace' in Ethiopian was a title. It was bestowed on the queen mother, whose position was laid down in institutional structures. She had a considerable political influence, but ruled only as regent, when her son was a minor. The mention of the Candace brings a touch of exotic colour into the narrative, following the model of classical accounts of travel and novels. Luke takes the opportunity 'to pick up here a theme that fascinated romantic spirits from about the middle of the first century, far into the second century. At least since the expedition to the Nile under Nero (61–62 CE), interest in Ethiopia had become so intense that a whole literature came into being to satisfy it.

One could write about this topic even when one had nothing substantially new to contribute.'[9]

Finally, we are told about the task entrusted to the eunuch as court official of the Candace: he was 'in charge of all her treasure' (v. 27), i.e. he was her finance minister or chancellor (the word which the German Catholic translation uses instead of 'eunuch'). The high position of this man is welcome to Luke, who wishes to show that the Christian message does not remain limited to the lower orders, but reaches even members of the upper classes. One might see this as a contradiction of Luke's tendency to be critical of wealth, which is equally present in his work. But we should note that such men as the eunuch or the chief tax-collector Zacchaeus (Lk 19:1–10), who is comparable to him, are not in fact members of the social class that would correspond to their position and wealth; besides this, it remains to be seen what they do with their riches in the service of the community, when they have become Christians.

Up to this point, the text contains no religious perspectives. Luke has kept these for the close of his presentation, where he tells us that the eunuch is a *visitor to Jerusalem* and a *reader of Isaiah*. Even in distant Ethiopia, the eunuch has heard something about Judaism from merchants and travellers; historically speaking, this is not at all implausible, when one bears in mind that there was a Jewish colony in the fifth and fourth centuries BCE on the island of Elephantine near Aswan on the Nile, not so very far to the north. His feelings for Judaism were so strong, and he found the Jewish faith so attractive, that he undertook the arduous journey to Jerusalem in order to pray in the temple there, perhaps on the occasion of one of the great pilgrimage feasts. But how close a relationship to Judaism was it possible for him to have? His physical condition presented a problem here, since the Law is unambiguous: 'He whose testicles are crushed or whose male member is cut off shall not enter the assembly of the Lord' (Deut 23:1). This regulation is maintained in Qumran, Josephus and Philo: 'The law . . . excludes from the sacred assembly all who are unworthy, beginning with the men . . . who falsify the distinctive mark bestowed on them by nature.'[10] Like Cornelius (Acts 10:2), eunuchs could enjoy only the status of a 'God-fearer' who sympathised with Judaism and made personal sacrifices for his religion, but for one reason or another either could not or did not take the step of a full conversion as a proselyte.[11] He was not allowed to go further than the court of the Gentiles in the temple at Jerusalem.

Despite the disappointment this may have caused him, the eunuch in our narrative did not lapse into hopelessness. On his return journey, he

---

[9] E. Plümacher, *Lukas als hellenistischer Schriftsteller*, 12f.

[10] *De specialibus legibus* ('On the individual Laws') 1, 324f.

[11] I have argued elsewhere that Luke already envisages this particular group in Lk 1–2: 'Gottesfürchtige im Magnificat?', *NTS* 43 (1997), 134–9.

is reading a scroll of Isaiah which he had with him. It is more likely to have been in Greek than in Hebrew, since he certainly knew Greek, and the quotation at vv. 32f. from Is 53:7f. follows the wording of the Greek Bible. If he continued only a few columns further, he would have found the following promise at Is 56:3–7:

> Let not the foreigner who has joined himself to the Lord say, 'The Lord will surely separate me from his people'; and let not the eunuch say, 'Behold, I am a dry tree.' For thus says the Lord: 'To the eunuchs who keep my sabbaths, who choose the things that please me and hold fast my covenant, I will give in my house and within my walls a monument and a name better than sons and daughters . . . these I will bring to my holy mountain, and make them joyful in my house of prayer; their burnt offerings and their sacrifices will be accepted on my altar; for my house shall be called a house of prayer for all peoples.'

This prospect is an eschatological promise, and therefore cannot suspend the regulations of the law. It remains oriented to the law and Jerusalem: the sabbath must be kept, and the eunuch and the foreigner can find salvation only in the house of the Lord in Jerusalem. At this point in the story, of course, the eunuch is in fact going in the opposite direction, away from Jerusalem to his own country. Nevertheless, this prophetic word opens up a perspective of hope, which will be fulfilled in Christianity for the castrated foreigner from Ethiopia.

b. Discussion about scripture and baptism

The detailed exposition in vv. 26–29 contains so many important pointers that it would suffice as a basis for determining the basic message of this entire passage, although in fact the main portion of the text is still to come. At the centre of this passage lies the quotation from scripture in vv. 32f., framed by the reflection in vv. 30f. on the problem of understanding, and by Philip's exposition in vv. 34f. Verses 36–38 then tell us about the baptism.

The scriptural passage which the eunuch is reading aloud (so that it is possible for Philip to hear it and identify it) comes from the fourth Servant Song (Is 53:7f.). It is exceedingly difficult to interpret this text, especially since the textually dubious Hebrew version and the Greek translation diverge from one another. Let us be content with following the christological directive which Luke gives the reader of this text in v. 35, when he has Philip proclaim the gospel of Jesus Christ on the basis of this scriptural passage. The words: 'As a sheep led to the slaughter or a lamb before its shearer is dumb, so he opens not his mouth' would then refer to Jesus' death on the cross, which he endured without resistance or protest. The words, 'In his humiliation his condemnation was removed', already point ahead to a reversal: the 'humiliation' summarises once again the entire event of the passion, while the removal of the unjust judgement passed against Jesus already indicates his rehabilitation by God, which takes place through the resurrection from the dead. 'Who can describe his generation?' is no longer, as in the original Hebrew text, a lamentation over the painful fact that the Servant of the Lord will not have any descendants, but is rather the expression of joy that Jesus Christ, as 'the first-born of many sisters and brothers' (Rom 8:29), will have the believers as his descendants, a progeny so numerous that it will no longer be possible to express them in words and count them. 'For his life is taken up from the earth' no longer implies only the death of Jesus, but the entire sequence of his being taken away or taken up (cf. Lk 9:51; Acts 1:9), which also includes the resurrection and ascension.

At the same time, the context also makes it possible to apply the scriptural quotation existentially to the eunuch: despite his high position, he has experienced humiliation of various kinds because of his physical condition, without being able to put up much resistance. He had to give up any hope of physical descendants; his life will not leave any trace here on earth. Now he can be sure that God raises up those who are humiliated, that spiritual progeny also counts, and that life can be preserved and saved in other ways than physical reproduction.

The eunuch asks at v. 31 where he can find a capable expositor who can initiate the processes of understanding which consist in opening up new possibilities of applying scripture, bringing its christological and existential meaning to light. There is an unmistakable similarity between this whole constellation (dialogue about scripture during a journey, christological application of scripture and implicit hermeneutical reflection) and the story of the disciples *en route* to Emmaus at Lk 24:13–35. Just as Philip continues the activity of the earthly Jesus at Acts 8:5–7 through his preaching and working of miracles, so here he takes on the role of the risen Lord as interpreter and expositor.

Clearly, the preparatory study of scripture, the conversation with Philip and the lengthy exegesis which Philip appends to the text (although Luke does not present this in detail: cf. v. 35) are sufficient preparation for baptism; no further pre-baptismal catechesis is required. Running water is immediately at hand. The eunuch asks if anything prevents him from receiving baptism, but no hindrances exist (v. 36), so baptism is administered in v. 38. This shocked later scribes so much that they inserted v. 37, which is banished to a footnote in modern translations: 'And Philip said, "If you believe with all your heart, you may [be baptised]." And he replied, "I believe that Jesus Christ is the Son of God".' Some manuscripts have a variant at v. 39: 'The Holy Spirit came over the eunuch, but the angel snatched Philip away.' In this way, missing elements from the baptismal liturgy—e.g. the profession of faith on the part of the catechumen and the reception of the Spirit—are supplied subsequently. The speedy baptism in Luke's original text, administered virtually without prior conditions, is however well suited to the atmosphere of miracles and providence in which the entire sequence of events is steeped.

But how does this individual narrative, precisely in view of its character as the account of a providential action, fit into the structure of Acts as a whole? Exegetes have often denied that it is a God-fearing Gentile who receives baptism here, since they hold that the universal mission to the Gentiles cannot begin until Paul, the Gentile missionary *par excellence*, comes on the scene. This does not happen until Acts 9; and even then it is not Paul who actually inaugurates the Gentile mission, still less Philip. It is only when Peter baptises Cornelius in Acts 10 that he officially initiates this mission. Thus the Ethiopian is made out to be a proselyte, one who can be counted among the throng of pious Jews and proselytes mentioned in Acts 2:5, 11. It is certainly important for Luke to emphasise strongly the Ethiopian's affinities to Judaism, something he also does in the case of Cornelius (see below); but to make the Ethiopian a proselyte is to misinterpret the strategy Luke is actually following. After he has presented the Samaritans, the God-fearers offer him a further transitional zone before he lets Paul have his first encounter with naked paganism, later and in another place.

The real significance of the pericope about the Ethiopian surely lies elsewhere. Let us recall that Ethiopia is on the boundaries of the earth, something that is not the case with Rome, where the Acts of the Apostles ends. Thus it is in fact only here—and nowhere else—that the final programmatic point from Acts 1:8 ('. . . and to the end of the earth') is genuinely fulfilled, in an act of prophetic anticipation. To speak of anticipation means that this goal has not yet truly been attained; the Christian message has reached only one inhabitant of that boundary region, while he (and it) were still close to Jerusalem. Thus, even after the close of Acts, the universal programme is rather far from realisation. Since this action by Philip initially has no ecclesiological consequences, it does not contradict the Cornelius episode: no community is founded. The Ethiopian returns to his native land, and we do not know what happens to him there (although Eusebius makes him the founder of the Christian Church in Ethiopia). We shall now go on to speak of the ecclesiological consequences of the events in the house of Cornelius.

A final point: Robert C. Tannehill has offered a plausible evaluation of the relationship between the evangelist Philip and the apostle Peter in the mission in Samaria and at the baptism of the God-fearer, arguing that Philip, as representative of the hellenist group, takes on the role of a pioneer, while the first apostles only just succeed in keeping up with him.[12]

---

[12] Since it is possible only to provide no more than a few individual references in the footnotes, let me explicitly state here that the presentation in this study owes a great deal to the narrative commentary by R.C. Tannehill, *Narrative Unity*, as well as to the studies by R. I. Pervo and the commentary of L. T. Johnson.

III

IN CAESAREA (ACTS 10–12)

1. *The baptism of Cornelius (Acts 10:1–11:18)*

The entire eighth chapter of the Acts of the Apostles, consisting of the two individual narratives which we have just studied, runs to about ninety lines in a Greek edition of the New Testament, while the Cornelius episode alone runs to 145. This fact alone suffices to show the programmatic significance which Luke attaches to this episode.[1] He invests even more care in his portrait of Cornelius than in that of the Ethiopian chamberlain, and he sets this passage in high relief by means of a number of compositional devices, not least the repetition in direct speech, in Peter's discourse at 11:5–17, of the entire sequence of events.

a. The centurion Cornelius and his household

We learn at Acts 10:1 that Cornelius served in the Roman army as a centurion of the Italian cohort. A cohort consisted of six detachments of one hundred men, each detachment under the command of its centurion, and the Italian cohort, an auxiliary unit made up of freedmen, was stationed in Syria and other territories in the first century CE. With his whole house, i.e. with all those who made up his family, Cornelius lived the life of a pious God-fearer. In other words, he followed the Jewish law as far as possible, as we see from the fact that he gave large sums to the Jewish people and prayed to God continuously. The angel confirms this when he says to him, in the opening vision: 'Your prayers and your alms have ascended as a memorial before God' (v. 4). The messengers whom he sends describe him to Peter as 'an upright and God-fearing man, who is well spoken of by the whole Jewish nation' (v. 22). In many respects, he resembles his 'twin brother' in Luke's two-volume work, the centurion at Capernaum in Lk 7:1–10, for whom the Jewish elders put in a good word with Jesus: 'He is worthy to have you do this for him, for he loves our nation, and he built us our synagogue' (Lk 7:3–5). In the case of Cornelius, Luke emphasises in addition that this evaluation applies to his whole household. The 'soldier from among those that waited on him', whom he sends with two domestic slaves as his envoy, is 'devout'

---

[1] Cf. A. Barbo, 'Cornelio (At 10, 1–11, 18): percorsi per una piena integrazione dei pagani nella Chiesa', in I. Cardellini (ed.), *Lo 'straniero' nella Bibbia: aspetti storici, istituzionali e teologici* (RStB 8, 1–2), Bologna 1996, 277–95; B. Witherington, *Acts*, 339–65.

(Acts 10:7), and the same will be true of Cornelius' relatives and closest friends, whom he summons to wait for Peter's visit (v. 24). This ideal family brings Peter to the insight 'that God shows no partiality, but in every nation any one who fears him and does what is right is acceptable to him' (vv. 34f.).

Once again, Luke chooses an especially noble Gentile from the group of God-fearers, an *anima naturaliter christiana* or *judaica*, in order to choke at source every conceivable objection to the Gentile mission. All potential or *de facto* opponents must join Peter in asking whether there exist any grounds whatever for refusing such people baptism: would not this mean opposing God? One might perhaps criticise Cornelius for not having made the full conversion to Judaism, but this was because his military job was not easily compatible with complete observance of the sabbath rest and of all the dietary taboos (to say nothing of circumcision, a painful operation for adults). This is also the sociological explanation of the genesis of the category of God-fearers, Gentiles who built up a network of close relationships to Judaism, to the synagogue community and to the Jewish faith in God; it is not unthinkable that the author himself, Luke, was one of these. Recently, scholars have disputed the existence of these persons, since concepts such as 'worshipper of God' or 'God-fearer' had not yet stabilised, terminologically speaking—these words could also cover pious Jews and proselytes. Indeed, this special group of Gentile God-fearers has been dismissed as a Lukan invention. But this is to throw the baby out with the bath-water. A lengthy Jewish inscription from Aphrodisias, listing a number of names of non-Jewish 'worshippers of God', has given renewed support to the traditional view.[2]

The sequence of events is set in train by a vision of Cornelius, which is reported a total of four times. First of all, in Acts 10:3–6, it is communicated in the narrative account: an angel of the Lord appears to Cornelius and charges him to fetch Peter from Joppa, without however explaining why Cornelius is to do this. This means that he is charged to accept this directive in confident trust. The account of the vision which the envoys of Cornelius give to Peter at 10:22 goes further. Despite its extreme brevity, this version contains a new element: the angel has also directed Cornelius to listen to what Peter has to tell him. At 10:30–32, Cornelius takes the opportunity to relate his vision to Peter in his own words; in v. 33, outside the framework of the account of his vision, he makes known his readiness 'to hear all that you have been commanded by the Lord'. Finally, Peter relates the vision of Cornelius before a further group of hearers in Jerusalem (11:13), giving it a new conclusion: 'He [i.e. Peter]

---

[2] Cf. J. Reynolds and R. Tannebaum, *Jews and Godfearers at Aphrodisias. Greek Inscriptions with Commentary* (Cambridge Philological Society. Supplementary Volume 12), Cambridge 1987; more recently, M. Reiser, 'Hat Paulus Heiden bekehrt?', *BZ* NF 39 (1995), 76–91 at 83–7.

will declare to you a message by which you will be saved, you and all your household' (11:14). Like a precious stone, the vision is turned this way and that, to discover new facets and refractions in the light. It is only in the continuous process of communication between human persons that the deeper meaning of the vision is disclosed—at the outset, it was anything but clear. One can also reverse the perspective, and try the experiment of reading the visions and utterances of the Spirit in this pericope as follows: it can be observed that complex processes, full of conflict, occur among human beings in their search for a decision, but that these processes lead to a good outcome. Retrospectively, it can be seen that the development made towards the correct goal, and was congruent with God's plan. Those who hand on the tradition have paid tribute to this insight by choosing conventional methods of presentation such as the account of a vision and of instructions by the Holy Spirit, since these means portray more directly God's hidden governance of events.

b. The encounter with Peter

Peter too, is carefully prepared at Acts 10:9–16 for his encounter with Cornelius, although he himself is initially unaware of this. Shortly before the messengers from Caesarea arrive, Peter goes up to the flat roof of the house at the midday hour to pray. In keeping with the time of day, he feels hunger—and suddenly he sees the answer to this hunger when the heaven opens and a strange container descends, like a linen cloth held at four corners, perhaps symbolising the four points of the compass or the ends of the world. In this cloth are four-footed animals, reptiles, birds and (as the second account adds at 11:6) wild animals. These are specimens of 'all', i.e. all known species, and this necessarily includes impure animals too. The formulation here recalls the creation of the animals in Gen 1:24f. and their rescue from the flood in Noah's ark (cf. Gen 6:20; 7:14). This by itself shows the theological structure which lies hidden beneath the text. All the animals were created by God, and all were rescued from destruction in the flood. If God cares in such a way for them, can it ever be right to make a distinction between pure and impure beasts, as the law does? A heavenly voice commands Peter to kill some of these animals and eat them, thus satisfying his hunger. Peter demurs vigorously: 'Never!' He has never yet eaten anything impure, and the danger of doing so appears too great (cf. Ezek 4:13f.). The heavenly voice instructs him: 'What God has cleansed, you must not call common.' This happens three times, and then the vision ceases as suddenly as it began. Peter remains puzzled (v. 17), uncertain what the vision might mean (v. 19). And yet, if one detaches it from its context, the meaning is surely rather obvious: the categories of pure and impure animals have lost their validity. One may eat all meat, without any distinction in view of its origin, and this applies also to Jews who profess their faith in Jesus the Messiah. This is presumably the original message of the vision, which justified this liberal attitude by appealing to Peter. But Luke directly avoids drawing this radical conclusion. We shall see later what he does with the vision.

In the meantime, Cornelius' envoys are standing below, at the door of the house of Simon the tanner in Joppa, where Peter is staying. Since the vision had told him nothing about them, it is now the Spirit who instructs him at vv. 19–20 to come down from the roof to the envoys and accompany them 'without making any distinction' or (following the majority of translations) 'without any reservations', i.e. without keeping his distance from them because of their Gentile provenance, as the law prescribed. Peter emphasises this point when he gives an account of what he has done: 'The Spirit told me to go with them, making no distinction' (11:12). Even as late as the apostolic council, he returns to this point, though here he argues in a different sense: God showed thereby that he himself 'made no distinction between us and them' (15:9). This 'lack of hesitation' is displayed first of all in the hospitality which Peter extends to the envoys in the house in which he himself is a guest (v. 23a).

Next morning, the group sets out on the road from Joppa to Caesarea. It is now considerably enlarged, because apart from Peter and the envoys of Cornelius, six Jewish Christian brethren from Joppa (cf. 11:12), who will be needed as witnesses, accompany them. When this delegation reaches Caesarea, Cornelius rushes to meet Peter and salutes him like a true messenger from heaven: he falls down before him and venerates him with a genuflection (in a religious context, the verb *proskynein*, which is employed here, is normally translated: 'he adored him'). This goes too far: Peter is obliged to protest, for there is a danger of the kind of misunderstanding we know from the story of Simon Magus, the 'great power of God' in human form. Peter is shocked, and demurs: 'Stand up; I too am a man' (v. 26). Here we recall that Peter reacts similarly in a Jewish context also, after the healing of the lame man at Acts 3:12–16: Why are you looking at us apostles, as if we had performed this miracle by means of our own power? It was the God of Abraham, Isaac and Jacob who worked through us, but in such a way that he remains clearly distinct from us, his human messengers.

When he finally enters the house, the first statement Peter makes (v. 28) is that he really ought not to be there at all, since it is forbidden for Jews to have close contacts with 'foreigners' (*allophylos* in Greek). But it is at this point that Luke introduces Peter's vision: God has shown him that one should not make a discrimination between pure and impure persons. The abolition of the distinction between pure and impure animals is interpreted anthropologically and socio-culturally as the abolition of the barriers that separate Jews and Gentiles. The central theme of the vision, eating, plays only a secondary role here, in that these barriers were erected above all to prevent table-fellowship. It was difficult, if not indeed quite impossible, for people to eat together, since the Jews would always be afraid of eating impure foods. Thus it is characteristic that the accusation raised against Peter at 11:3 is: 'Why did you go to uncircumcised men and eat with them?' In the case of Cornelius, we may certainly suppose that he was an experienced 'God-fearer', aware of Jewish sensibilities, and that he was perfectly capable of guaranteeing Jewish visitors a pure house and pure meals. At any rate, the theme of eating does not recur in Acts 11:4–18. In the long run, the failure to tackle it in depth was not a sustainable position.

Peter begins his sermon in 10:34–43 with an introduction related to the immediate situation: God does not favour one person over another in partisan fashion. Although he holds to the precedence of Israel in salvation history, since it was to this people that the earthly Jesus addressed his proclamation of peace, Peter opens up a universal perspective by means of the christological predicate at the end of the verse: this Jesus Christ is lord of all. He continues with a brief summary of the whole gospel in a few verses, parts of which recall the later creed: crucified (v. 39), risen from the dead on the third day (v. 40), judge of the living and the dead (v. 42), forgiveness of sins (v. 43).

c. The consequences

Before Peter has finished his discourse, the Spirit descends on all his non-Jewish hearers (v. 44) and they begin to speak in tongues and praise God (v. 46). The believers 'from among the circumcised', i.e. the brethren from Joppa who have accompanied Peter, are astonished (v. 45) and note that the Spirit is poured out *even* over Gentiles. This 'even' is a link back to the first outpouring of the Spirit in Jerusalem at Pentecost, and Peter underlines this both in v. 47—they 'have received the Holy Spirit just as we have'—and *a fortiori* in 11:15: 'the Holy Spirit fell on them just as on us at the beginning'. In other words, what happens here is something of the highest theological importance. It is the Pentecost Feast of the Gentiles. After the Jewish Christian Church at the beginning, the universal Church consisting of both Jews and Gentiles is now founded. The numerous directive signals given in the text by the angel, by the heavenly voice, and by the Spirit, aim at this outpouring of the Spirit and culminate in it. Clearly, however, an overwhelming demonstration of this nature was needed, in order to carry through the integration of the Gentiles into the Church.

Before they can be full members of the Church, they must be baptised; in this case, baptism follows the reception of the Spirit. Peter interprets the working of the Spirit correctly and orders that Cornelius, his family and his friends be baptised at once (v. 47). Apparently, he does not do so himself. Rather, it is his companions from Joppa who perform this action, thereby creating a spiritual bond between the future neighbouring communities. Nor should we overlook the seemingly insignificant concluding information: 'Then they asked him to remain for some days' (v. 48). Peter and his companions certainly grant this request and stay in the Gentile Christian house, so that the new house Church in Caesarea embodies for the first time the Church of Jews and Gentiles. Here it is born, here it becomes a reality. Let us add that the formation of this entire tradition begins with the historical knowledge that the house Church of Cornelius was the first Christian foundation in Caesarea, from which the Christian community there developed.

When we look back at this narrative, we observe that it involves not only *one* conversion, but several. It is not only the Gentile centurion Cornelius, whose transition to Christianity takes place with surprising smoothness, who is converted; Peter too, who had held aloof hitherto from everything impure, must be converted, as must his Jewish companions. And finally, his fellow apostles and the brethren in Jerusalem must also be converted. Peter succeeds in overcoming their initial resistance by means of his detailed account of events. At the close, they agree with him and sanction the decision that he has taken on his own.

One may have the impression that Luke drops the narrative thread altogether at 11:19–24, but he himself sees this section as part of the consequences of these events. He returns at 11:19 to the great persecution mentioned at 8:1. Some of those who had been scattered at that time (and were hellenists, since they had originally come from Cyprus and Cyrene to Jerusalem) come as far as Antioch, where they preach the gospel to the Greeks too and win many of them for the faith. There is a point to Luke's narrative juxtaposition and sequence of events. The groups of hellenists around Stephen and Philip had in fact taken an earlier and independent decision in favour of the Gentile mission, but Luke wishes to subordinate this to Peter and the first apostles, who are to function as a model for this mission. It is not without reason (even though he actually finds no reason for complaint) that Barnabas journeys from Jerusalem at 11:22 in order to see that all is well in Antioch.

d. Looking ahead to the apostolic council

A direct trajectory leads from the birth of the community in Antioch to the apostolic council, which could more accurately be called a synod, held in Jerusalem to discuss the Gentile mission. Luke's compositional technique attaches special weight to this meeting by placing it in the centre of his Acts of the Apostles (ch. 15). Representatives of a strict Jewish Christian faction want to introduce circumcision for Gentile Christians in Antioch (15:1) and hence in principle for all such converts (15:5). This gives rise to a dispute which must be settled by the assembly in Jerusalem. James, the brother of the Lord and future leader of the

Jerusalem community, makes a vital contribution by quoting a text from Amos (8:11f.) which yields the desired meaning only in the Greek version: the ruined hut of David will be restored when all—even the Gentile nations—seek the Lord. It follows that it is not necessary for them to be received formally by means of circumcision into Israel, the people of salvation (15:16–19).

A number of specific historical and exegetical problems arise here. What traditions has Luke worked on? How is his account related to that of Paul at Gal 2:1–10? What factors should guide us in dating the 'council'? There is no space here to discuss these questions in detail; what interests us is the relationship between the Cornelius episode and the apostolic council. Is it not natural to suppose that this matter was settled in principle at 11:18? This is what Peter appears to feel, since his contribution to the debate (15:7–11) consists almost exclusively of reminiscences of Caesarea, where God himself gave the impetus for the baptism of Gentiles by pouring out the Spirit. Anyone who opposes this is putting God to the test.

It is not at all improbable, historically speaking, that Jewish pressure on the Jerusalem community had increased in the interval, so that the dominant tendency now inclined to a strict observance of the law. But this does not explain the difficulties of Luke's composition. Let us be content with one observation, which finds its starting-point in a problematic feature of the narrative about Cornelius. As I have written above, eating in common was not really discussed at that time. Peter's vision, which originally tended in a radical direction, could have provided the occasion for tackling this issue, but it had not been settled in depth. It is unlikely that all the Gentile converts since then were God-fearers like Cornelius, in whose house these problems did not arise; this, however, entails a profound change in the the initial situation, as far as the Jewish-Christian side is concerned. It is one thing to baptise Gentiles without demanding circumcision; it is quite another to regulate the subsequent common life. For example, were Jewish Christians now obliged to pay deference to baptised Gentiles by eating impure foods, without any distinctions at all? Most of those concerned answered this question with an unambiguous negative. Paul had to fight against this view in the controversy at Antioch (Gal 2:11–14). Despite his energetic counter-arguments, he did not win the day.

It became clear in the course of time that decisions on questions of principle, no matter how august these might be, taken by majorities and formally ratified, are no substitute for individual regulations. This is why James' ordinances are reported at 15:20, 29 as the substantial fruit of the assembly. Gentiles who become Christians are to refrain (1) from eating meat offered to idols, (2) from fornication (including marriage within forbidden degrees of relationship), (3) from what is strangled (i.e. from the meat of animals which had not been slaughtered in accordance with the prescriptions of the law), and (4) from blood, which refers less to the drinking of blood than to eating meat that contained traces of blood. These ordinances hark back to the regulations in Lev 17–18 for foreigners who lived in Israel and were not required to observe the whole of the law. Minimum requirements were made, to ensure that they and the Israelites could live and prosper together. In a very similar manner, James' ordinances intend to indicate how strictly observant Jewish Christians and Gentile Christians can live alongside one another in mixed communities such as those in Syria. Here we should note where the addressees of the letter lived: v. 23 tells us that it was sent 'to the brethren who are of the Gentiles in Antioch and Syria and Cilicia'.

We should note that the decree does not clash with Peter's vision in Acts 10, as would have been the case if it had prescribed the direct discrimination between pure and impure animals which is found in the Old Testament law. Nevertheless, this categorisation sneaks in by the back door, since it is virtually unthinkable that anyone would start to practise the ritual slaughter of impure animals: meat from ritually slaughtered animals surely always came from pure beasts. But the decree is limited both geographically and temporally—not only for us, for whom the decree has lost its validity, but already for Luke himself. A compromise was reached for one specific period of time, which was no longer Luke's own period, and one specific region, which is not coterminous with the area of Paul's subsequent mission. This compromise makes possible the unhindered subsequent development of missionary activity, thereby also preserving the unity of the Church.

It must be pointed out that a genuine dilemma is presented at this point: the kind of considerations involved in the decree would be genuinely superfluous only in communities consisting exclusively of Gentile Christians, with no Jewish Christian members at all. But one cannot be happy with this final outcome of the general development; theoretically speaking, it ought to be possible for a Christian to observe voluntarily the Jewish dietary prescriptions or, in somewhat milder form, at least the ordinances of James' decree. This observation should not be dismissed as a mere intellectual game. It very quickly acquires practical importance for the small Jewish-Christian communities which are endeavouring to develop their own lifestyle in the modern state of Israel.

2. Herod Agrippa I (Acts 12:20–23)[3]

A new disaster threatens the Jerusalem community in Acts 12, when King Herod makes a name for himself as its persecutor. He kills the

---

[3] Cf. O. W. Allen Jr., *The Death of Herod. The Narrative and Theological Function of Retribution in Luke–Acts* (SBL.DS 158), Atlanta 1997; A. Brent, 'Luke–Acts and the Imperial Cult in Asia Minor', *JThS* NS 48 (1997), 411–38.

apostle James with the sword (12:1f.), and when the Jewish populace applauds him for this, he throws Peter too into prison (12:3). Peter is however freed in a miraculous manner. A reader without specialist knowledge may be uncertain about who this King Herod was, but the blame attaches to some extent to Luke himself. We must therefore begin by looking at the historical context as a whole.

a. The Herodian dynasty and Luke's two-volume work

The narrative in Luke's Gospel begins, after the prologue, with the words: 'In the days of Herod, king of Judaea' (Lk 1:5). This is the introduction to the 'prehistory', i.e. the conception and birth of John the Baptist and of Jesus. The ruler mentioned here is Herod the Great (37–4 BCE), the ancestor and founder of the Herodian ruling dynasty.

Herod had several sons, and the region over which he ruled was divided among them, so that each became 'tetrarch' or ruler over a quarter of the territory. One of these sons, Herod Antipas, was tetrarch over Galilee and Peraea from 4 BCE to 39 CE (Lk 3:1) and hence the sovereign of Jesus of Nazareth. At Lk 3:19f., he imprisons John the Baptist, and Lk 9:9 tells us that he had him beheaded. The specifically Lukan material also relates that Pilate sent Jesus to be interrogated by Herod Antipas (Lk 23:6–12).

Herod Antipas was the uncle and brother-in-law of Agrippa I, son of Aristobulus, who was himself a son of Herod the Great. Thanks to his personal friendship with the emperor Caligula, he acquired the tetrarchies of Philip and Antipas; the emperor Claudius added Samaria and Judaea to these territories, since Agrippa had helped him to consolidate his rule. The result was that Agrippa succeeded in reigning from 41 to 44 CE as 'the last king of Judaea' over a territory as large as that of Herod the Great.[4] During his reign, he made a great show of programmatic loyalty to the Law and of piety. Ultimately, we do not know whether this was more for tactical reasons than because of personal conviction. His people noted this with pleasure. Nevertheless, historically speaking, he was not the notorious scoundrel we meet in Acts; the picture in Josephus is more differentiated. This Agrippa is the persecutor of Christians mentioned in Acts 12. In our other sources, he is always referred to only as (Julius) Agrippa, never as Herod, whereas Luke consistently refers to him as Herod, never as Agrippa; Luke often calls Antipas the 'tetrarch' (e.g. at Acts 13:1), but he never gives Agrippa this title. This is not because of a lack of historical knowledge, but because Luke has a precise purpose here. Just as Herod Antipas has John executed, so Herod Agrippa has James executed. These two members of the Herodian ruling dynasty

---

[4] Detailed information in D. R. Schwartz, *Agrippa I: The Last King of Judaea* (TSAJ 23), Tübingen 1990.

embody the figure of the tyrant who inflicts bloody persecution on the true worshippers of God.

At Acts 25:13–26:32, Paul is given the opportunity to defend his case before another King Herod, this time Agrippa II, a son of Agrippa I. In 53 CE, he had received the tetrarchy which had earlier belonged to Philip. This permits us to make a rather remarkable observation: Luke's two-volume work, from its beginning at Lk 1:5 to its close shortly after Acts 26, is embedded in a chronological framework spanning four generations of the Herodian royal family, from the founder, Herod the Great, to his great-grandson Agrippa II. This may of course be regarded as a coincidence, due to the situation of the times, but one may also perceive the insight that the history of Jesus and the history of Christianity do not take place in a vacuum, but are inseparably interlocked with the history of the Jewish people and with secular history.

b. Luke's account of Herod's death

After his failed attempt on Peter's life, Herod withdraws to Caesarea by the sea (Acts 12:19). He now falls into a great rage (v. 20) against the towns of Tyre and Sidon on the Phoenician coast; these lay outside his own dominions, and it is possible that he was carrying on a trade war with them. The two cities fear for their supplies of corn and food, which came from Agrippa's kingdom, and they send an embassy to make an offer of peace. They play safe by preparing the terrain in advance: they 'persuade' the royal chamberlain, Blastus, no doubt by means of a large gift of money. It appears that the peace treaty is to be proclaimed with solemnity on an appointed day (v. 21). Herod clothes himself in his royal robes for the occasion, takes his seat on the throne and makes an oration. His audience—the envoys, his courtiers, and some of the (Gentile) population of the city—cry out in praise: 'The voice of a god, and not of man!' (v. 22).

This acclamation obviously does not mean that the king had a 'divine' tenor voice or an especially warm baritone. He is praised because the crowd believe that they can sense the divine power and the divine being in his person. He promises peace, he bestows benefactions, he behaves kindly and mercifully, just like a real god. Here we encounter once again the phenomenon of a 'divine man' in the setting of the classical cult of rulers. This had developed from 400 BCE onwards on the dual basis of the older cult of heroes, i.e. the divinisation of outstanding personalities after their death, and of the ceremonial expressions of gratitude to benefactors in Asia Minor and Greece. It found a point of crystallisation in the figure of Alexander the Great and it was especially promoted and developed into a unified imperial cult by Alexander's successor kings in Egypt and Syria. The genuine cult of rulers entails the offering of sacrifices to the living king, as well as the erection of temples and statues and the foundation of festal games. The expression of honour paid to Herod Agrippa seems modest, in comparison to all this; it scarcely goes beyond an exaggerated flattery.

Nevertheless, retribution follows at once. Herod Agrippa did not react energetically enough in rejecting this idea; rather, he accepted the flattery and thereby broke the first commandment, 'I am the Lord, your God. You shall have no other gods before me' (Ex 20:2f.), and transgressed against the Jewish profession of faith, 'Hear, O Israel: the Lord our God is one Lord' (Deut 6:4). Verse 23 notes in lapidary fashion that he has failed to give God the honour that belongs to him alone. At once he is smitten by an angel of the Lord, an angel of punishment as in the Book of Exodus (cf. Ex 12:23), and he expires. However, he does not die quite so simply as that. We are not spared the revolting details: the king is eaten by worms while still alive. The appearance of a corpse in decomposition, swarming with maggots and worms, is here projected on to a living man.

This is a typical motif in classical literature, both secular and biblical. Godless men and foes of God, wicked tyrants and oppressors of the people of Israel meet a terrible end.[5] Luke himself has a further example of this, namely the death of Judas Iscariot: 'Falling headlong, he burst open in the middle and all his bowels gushed out' (Acts 1:18). He may have found a model for such passages in the long narrative of the death of Antiochus IV Epiphanes at 2 Macc 9:4–10. This king 'was seized with a pain in his bowels for which there was no relief and with sharp internal tortures', and 'the ungodly man's body swarmed with worms'. This case is particularly significant, because we know how Antiochus IV did in fact die. His death in a campaign against the Persians was indeed unexpected and premature, but it was far from being so spectactular as the elaborations of the legend.

c. Comparison with Flavius Josephus

We owe our historical knowledge about Agrippa I chiefly to Books 18 and 19 of the *Jewish Antiquities* by Flavius Josephus. It is worth comparing his longer version of the end of Agrippa's life with the shorter account by Luke. Josephus writes (*Ant.* 19, 343–350):

[343] After he had exercised sovereignty over the whole of Judea for three years, Agrippa now went to Caesarea, the former tower of Strato. Here he staged plays in honour of Caesar, since he knew that festal days for Caesar's well-being were being celebrated just then. A great number of respectable and important Jews from the entire province gathered for these festivities.

---

[5] See the material presented in the section: 'Das Ende des Gottlosen: Variationen eines Themas', in H.-J. Klauck, *Judas—ein Jünger des Herrn* (QD 111), Freiburg im Breisgau 1987, 116–21.

[344] Early on the morning of the second day, Agrippa went in a robe made with extraordinary skill from pure silver to the theatre, where the first rays of the sun lit up the silver with a shimmering gleam, so blinding that the onlookers turned their eyes away in terror. [345] At once, his flatterers cried out to him from every side, calling him a god and saying, 'Have mercy on us! Hitherto we have revered you only as a human being, but in future we shall worship a supernatural being in you.' [346] The king did not rebuke them for this, nor reject their blasphemous flatteries. But when he looked away immediately after this, he saw an owl above his head, sitting on a rope, and recognised this as a messenger of his doom. Once before, a messenger had brought the news of his good fortune [cf. *Ant.* 18, 201]; now it was an indication of his imminent death, filling him with bitter sorrow. Soon, he felt fierce pains in his body too, which tortured him in an unheard-of manner from the very outset of his illness. [347] Then he turned his gaze on his friends and said to them, 'Behold, I—your god—must now leave this life, and fate cloaks in shame the meretricious brilliance of your words. You called me immortal, yet death is already stretching out its arms to receive me. But I must bear my destiny, as God wills. For I did not live in wretched circumstances, but rather in the highest splendour.' [348] While he was still speaking these words, his torments intensified to the highest degree. He was brought speedily into his palace, and the rumour soon spread that the king was dying. [349] At once, the entire people, with their wives and children, prostrated themselves on carpets (as is the custom of their ancestors) to beseech God that the king might recover, with wailing and lamentations on every side. The king, for his part, lay in a lofty room from which he could see the people lying on the ground, and he could not hold back his tears. [350] He endured the pain in his intestines for a further five days, until finally death released him. He died in the fifty-fourth year of his life and the seventh of his rule.

Some elements in Josephus seem more plausible, and some hints in Luke are easier to understand when one knows Josephus: the date of the festivities, i.e. the athletic contests founded by Herod the Great in honour of the Roman emperor, which were held every four years; the place where the action is set, viz. the theatre; and the motif of the splendid royal robe which provokes the flattery, in Josephus' account, when it is lit up by the sun's rays. Josephus does not mention the king's beautiful voice, the embassy from Tyre and Sidon, or Blastus the chamberlain. The punishing angel in Luke can be compared with the messenger of doom, the owl, in Josephus, which is also called *angelos* in Greek. In Josephus, the king has time to come to his senses and admit that he has over-reached himself. His sin does not diminish the devotion of his people, who pray for him and lament his misfortune. Both Josephus and Luke agree about the fact of his death. Josephus does not mention worms that eat up his body, but he does provide indications that allow a medical diagnosis; scholars have proposed an acute appendicitis, a heart attack, or a perforated ulcer. Here too we see where the legend begins and how it grows. The premature and painful death of the king prompted the question whether he was being punished by the judgement of God for his lack of reservation *vis-à-vis* incipient manifestations of the ruler cult.

Let us make one further point about the relationship between Luke and Josephus. Some scholars hold that Luke had read Josephus' writings. Since Josephus wrote the *Antiquities* after 95 CE, this would mean a relatively late date for the composition of Acts. This passage, however, does not favour such a thesis. One might indeed suppose that Luke had invented the worms as an additional detail, adding the beautiful voice for a reason which we shall discuss below. But where did he get the conflict with Tyre and Sidon, and the chamberlain Blastus, not mentioned in Josephus? What led him to go beyond Josephus and introduce precisely these details into his shortened version? When we consider both the differences and the agreement in many details of the information in the two accounts, it is surely better to suppose the existence of a common source on which Luke and Josephus independently drew.

d. Concealed criticism of the imperial cult?

It is not at all easy to determine correctly the function of this little episode in Luke's text. Most attempts at an explanation go no further than saying that, in the context of Acts 12, Herod Agrippa is now punished for his persecution of the Christian apostles and that this is intended as a warning to all enemies of the Christians. But does this go far enough? Is not the elaboration of the episode disproportionate, if nothing more is intended? Above all, one is left wondering about the role of the beautiful voice, a striking detail peculiar to Luke's account.

The hellenistic ruler cult was in fact no longer particularly relevant at the time of Herod Agrippa (*c*.40 CE) and the time when Acts was written (*c*.80–90 CE), since it had been replaced by the Roman imperial cult. Indeed, it would probably have been dangerous for oriental rulers, who were dependent on Rome, to attempt to compete with the imperial cult. There was however one Roman emperor who was utterly convinced of the beauty of his voice, and who pondered whether it would not be better for him to earn his living as an actor and singer: the emperor Nero.[6] Tacitus writes in his Annals that he had companions 'whose task it was day and night to make a din with their applause, attributing divine names to the beautiful figure of the prince and to his voice' (14.15, 8). Nero accused one senator 'of never having offered sacrifice for the well-being

---

[6] This point has already been seen, and illustrated with valuable material, by S. Lösch, *Deitas Jesu und antike Apotheose. Ein Beitrag zur Exegese und Religionsgeschichte*, Rottenburg 1933, 18–24.

of the prince or for his divine voice' (16.22, 1). Here we should also hear the testimony of the historian Dio Cassius, who describes the following scene in his *Roman History* (62[61].20, 4–6):

> After the emperor had passed through the circus and crossed the forum, accompanied in this manner by the soldiers, the knights and the senators, he ascended to the Capitol and then entered his palace. The entire city was decked with garlands, while all the populace cried out in chorus—with the senators forming an especially loud choir—'Hail to you, victor of the Olympian Games! Hail, victor of the Pythian Games! Augustus! Hail, Nero, our Hercules! Hail, Nero, our Apollo! The sole victor of the grand tour! The One who alone is from the beginning of time! Augustus! Augustus! Divine voice! Blessed are those permitted to hear you!'

Luke knew that his protagonist, Paul, had been executed at Rome in the time of the emperor Nero (it is true that Paul is still alive at the close of Acts, but his farewell discourse at 20:17–33, and the moving reaction at 20:36–38, show clearly enough the fact of his death). This locates the emperor Nero alongside Herod Antipas and Herod Agrippa. Each ruler in turn is responsible for a violent death: of John the Baptist, of James, and of Paul. And Nero too was punished by a dishonourable early death.

It would certainly have been imprudent to criticise an emperor directly, and it would also have confused the programme of political apologetics which Luke otherwise carries out; he concedes that the Roman authorities normally behave correctly towards the Christians. But even this apologetics has its limits, and bitterness finds release in hidden criticism (cf. also Lk 4:5f.). There was in fact only one ruler who was acclaimed for his 'beautiful voice', and the informed reader did not need further enlightenment. The admonition of the Gospel holds true here: 'He who has ears to hear, let him hear' (Lk 8:8).

IV

THE FIRST MISSIONARY JOURNEY (ACTS 13–14)

Up to this point, we have met the evangelist Philip and the apostle Peter, but we have not yet encountered the real protagonist of the Acts of the Apostles, Paul or Saul. But from now on, our concern will lie almost exclusively with him. We could choose to trace the path of Saul through our text, from his first appearance as a peripheral figure at the martyrdom of Stephen, where the witnesses deposit their clothes at his feet (Acts 7:58), via his activity as persecutor, his conversion and his various periods of residence in Damascus, Jerusalem, Caesarea and his home-town Tarsus (9:19–31), until he comes to live in Antioch. We should also have to pay attention here to Barnabas, a Cypriot (4:36) who was active in Jerusalem. He brought Saul to Antioch (11:26) and was his close companion, or rather his senior partner at the beginning; he took the newcomer by the hand and accompanied him in his first steps. However, we limit ourselves to noting the passage immediately preceding ch. 13. At 11:30, the community in Antioch send Barnabas and Saul to Jerusalem with a sum of money which they have collected for the needy sisters and brothers in Judaea. Clearly, they experience at close quarters the events in Jerusalem related in ch. 12. In the final verse of this chapter (12:25), they return to Antioch after fulfilling their task, together with John Mark, whom they bring with them from Jerusalem (cf. 12:12).

This passage is immediately followed at 13:1–3 by the description of life in the Antiochene community. We are given a list of five prophets and teachers who are active there, with Barnabas mentioned first and Saul last. The Holy Spirit charges them to set aside Barnabas and Saul for a special work. After preparatory fasting, the two are commissioned in an act of community worship with prayers and the laying on of hands. Thus begins the first missionary journey in Acts 13–14.

This first missionary journey poses questions about the transmission of tradition and about history and chronology, e.g. whether Luke is correct to place it before the apostolic council, or whether it actually took place only after this meeting (with which the journey to Jerusalem by Paul and Barnabas in Acts 11–12 would be linked). We shall not discuss such questions in detail here. It is sufficient for our purposes to note that even so severe a critic as Gerd Lüdemann affirms: 'The missionary journey with stations at Derbe, Lystra, Iconium, and

Antioch [in Pisidia] is an historical fact.'[1] The reversed order of cities in Lüdemann's list might be intended to suggest that Paul had started this missionary journey from his home-town Tarsus, to the east of Derbe. It is not without reason that Lüdemann omits any mention of Cyprus. According to 11:19, hellenists from Jerusalem had already done active missionary work on Cyprus, though preaching only to Jews. At 15:39, Barnabas, who came from the island, leaves for Cyprus with John Mark, who may have been his nephew (cf. Col 4:10), on a pastoral journey. Thus it is possible that the mission on Cyprus should be attributed to Barnabas alone, with the consequence that the punitive miracle at Acts 13:6–12 would originally have been performed by him and attached to Paul only at a secondary stage—an assessment occasionally found in the secondary literature, and sometimes extended to include the healing miracle at Lystra in 14:8–12. If however one accepts as historically correct the picture of Barnabas as initially the senior partner, there is no implausibility in assuming that he took Paul along with him on this enterprise. The only question still open is whether this was one journey, or the itineraries of two journeys compressed by Luke into a single account.

It is easy to follow the first stations of the journey on a map. From their home base, Antioch in Syria, Barnabas and Saul make for the nearest harbour, Seleucia, where they board a ship and sail for Cyprus, reaching Salamis on the eastern edge of the island (13:4f.). There 'they proclaimed the word of God in the synagogues of the Jews' (v. 5). Other literary sources and some modest archaeological discoveries attest the presence of a Jewish diaspora on Cyprus. Luke presents a stereotyped narrative: Paul always begins in the synagogue, turning to the Gentiles only when he is rejected there. A little later, at 13:46, Luke has Paul affirm, 'It was necessary that the word of God should be spoken first to you. Since you thrust it from you, and judge yourselves unworthy of eternal life, behold, we turn to the Gentiles.' The Jewish synagogue was the ideal point of contact for Jewish-Christian missionaries who came to a city where they knew no one. Here they could also meet open-minded Gentiles, and they could 'poach' such people from the synagogue; this naturally led to acute conflicts. This is the social-historical background to Luke's construction; to this we must add Paul's own view of the pre-eminent position of Israel in salvation history (cf. Rom 1:16, 'to the Jew first and also to the Greek'), which Luke clothes in stereotype narrative form.

---

[1] G. Lüdemann, *Das frühe Christentum,* 171; on what follows, cf. also J. Taylor, *Les Actes,* 127–95; C. Breytenbach, *Paulus und Barnabas in der Provinz Galatien. Studien zu Apostelgeschichte 13f.; 16,6; 18,23 und den Adressaten des Galaterbriefes* (AGJU 38), Leiden 1996.

1. *In Paphos on Cyprus (Acts 13:4–12)*[2]

Barnabas and Paul still have Mark with them for a short period (Acts 13:5); he will leave them when they continue their journey in Asia Minor (13:13). From Salamis, they journey to Paphos, about one hundred kilometres away on the west corner of the island; this was the capital city and the seat of the Roman administration. Here they meet not only the Roman proconsul Sergius Paulus, who displays interest in the proclamation of the gospel, but also a Jewish magician named Bar-Jesus, who belongs to the proconsul's entourage. Paul is the clear victor of the ensuing conflict with Bar-Jesus, who is struck blind and can no longer see the light of the sun, though only 'for a time'.

What is the literary genre of this remarkable narrative? Elements of a punitive miracle (cf. the death of Ananias and Sapphira in Acts 5:1–11) dominate especially the second half. 13:10–11a presents the wonder-working word of Paul, the protagonist, and v. 11b confirms and demonstrates the miracle that has taken place, viz. the sudden blindness of Bar-Jesus and the astonished reaction of the public in the person of Sergius Paulus. In the attempt to define the type of text to which the narrative as a whole belongs, we should also bear in mind stories of contests between competing magicians. Not only are these well attested in the popular traditions of many cultures (and in modern mythology: cf. the good magician Gandalf and the evil magician Saruman in the great classic of fantasy literature, J. R. R. Tolkien's *Lord of the Rings*); the Old Testament and early Christian literature are likewise familiar with them. We recall the struggle between Moses and the Egyptian magicians in Exodus (Ex 7–8), between Elijah and the priests of Baal on Mount Carmel (1 Kgs 18), between Daniel and the priests of Bel (Dan 14 LXX), or, as mentioned above, the duel between the apostle Peter and Simon Magus in the apocryphal Acts of Peter. We scarcely need mention who wins in each of these cases.

Our primary interest here is the portrait of the two central figures in our narrative, Bar-Jesus and Saul/Paul.

a. The sketch of Bar-Jesus

As with Simon Magus and the Ethiopian, Luke tells us a number of things about Paul's opponent in Paphos. First of all, he describes him in v. 6 as a *magician*.[3] We need not dwell here on this term; we refer to

---

[2] On the following textual passage, cf. especially L. Tosco, *Pietro e Paolo ministri del giudizio di Dio. Studio del genere letterario e della funzione di At 5,1–11 e 13,4–12* (RivBib Suppl 19), Bologna 1989; S.-Ch. Lin, *Wundertaten*, 19–145.

[3] Cf. J. J. Kilgallen, 'Acts 13,4–12: the role of the "*magos*"', *EstBib* 55 (1997), 223–37.

what was said about Simon Magus above. We recall that this word was reserved, on the basis of its Persian origin, to wise men from a priestly caste. It can be used in a neutral manner to designate astrologers, interpreters of dreams, soothsayers, healers and workers of miracles, but it also has the negative connotation of charlatan, trickster, mountebank or con man. The title 'guru', which likewise comes from the east, possesses a similar ambivalence today. Luke notes only the sombre reverse side of the term, employing it as a weapon to discredit opponents of whom he disapproves.

Luke adds a second attribute, that of *false prophet*, evoking traditions from the Old Testament which tell of the true prophet who speaks and acts as God's messenger and of the false prophets who contradict him, speaking in their own name and acting to their own advantage. It suffices here to look at a lengthy text like Jer 29:9–32, which gathers in one single passage all the standard elements of polemic. It is often given the heading 'Against the false prophets' in translations of the Bible:

> . . . [11] Both prophet and priest are ungodly; even in my house I have found their wickedness, says the Lord. [12] Therefore their way shall be to them like slippery paths in the darkness, into which they shall be driven and fall [this is to be the fate of Bar-Jesus in the future!], for I will bring evil upon them in the year of their punishment . . . [14] But in the prophets of Jerusalem I have seen a horrible thing: they commit adultery and walk in lies; they strengthen the hands of evildoers, so that no one turns from his wickedness . . . [16] Do not listen to the words of the prophets who prophesy to you, filling you with vain hopes; they speak visions of their own minds, not from the mouth of the Lord . . . [21] I did not send the prophets, yet they ran; I did not speak to them, yet they prophesied . . . [25] I have heard what the prophets have said who prophesy lies in my name, saying, 'I have dreamed, I have dreamed!' . . . [27] they think to make my people forget my name by their dreams which they tell one another, even as their fathers forgot my name for Baal . . . [32] Behold, I am against those who prophesy lying dreams, says the Lord, and who tell them and lead my people astray by their lies and their recklessness, when I did not send them or charge them; so they do not profit this people at all, says the Lord.

It is probable that Bar-Jesus also specialised in such matters as the interpretation of dreams and other forms of predicting the future. The punishment inflicted on him in v. 11, viz. that he is no longer to see the light of the sun, may be an indication that he also practised astrology: he would require the sun for his calculations.

The third thing we are told about Bar-Jesus is that he is a *Jew*. This is not so surprising as it may at first seem, since the title 'false prophet', drawn from the Old Testament, has already pointed in this direction. We ought not to imagine the Judaism of the first century of the Common Era as a monolithic orthodox block; it was not wholly free from tendencies to integrate popular and unorthodox religious practices. The Greek magical papyri include a number of Hebrew or Aramaic spells and sacred names, and the old Jewish woman with her spells and magic potions is a standard figure for Roman satirists such as Juvenal. A further example is provided by the Roman philosopher and rhetor Apuleius, who was obliged to defend himself before a court in North Africa in 158/159 CE against a charge of sorcery. He says in his defence that, if this were true, this would mean that he aimed at being 'a Carmendas or Damigeron or Moses or Jannes or Apollobex or Dardarius—or any other celebrated sorcerer you can name after Zoroaster and Ostanes' (90.5). The Jewish figures Moses and Jannes and the Persians Zoroaster and Ostanes in this quotation show that it was supposed that the most successful magicians with foreign names were to be found in the east. Flavius Josephus knows of a magician from Cyprus whom the Roman governor of Judaea asks for help (*Ant.* 20, 142):

> Felix, the governor of Judaea, had no sooner seen the exceedingly beautiful Drusilla, than he burned with love for her. Accordingly, he sent to her a Jew named Atomos, a friend of his who came from Cyprus and made himself out to be a magician, so that he might persuade her to leave her husband . . .

The next thing we learn is this man's proper name: *Bar-Jesus*. This too should astound us. 'Jesus' is indeed a common Jewish name, which we find even in the New Testament for persons other than Jesus Christ (cf. Col 4:11, 'Jesus who is called Justus'); the same is true in general also for the use of so-called patronymics, i.e. proper names which contain the father's name compounded with the Hebrew *ben* as in Benjamin, or the Aramaic *bar* as in Bar Kochba—both mean 'son'. Luke seems to be especially fond of this combination, since he not only mentions Barabbas, 'the son of the father' (!) in his passion narrative (Lk 23:18), but also Barnabas, interpreted in popular etymology to mean 'son of consolation' (Acts 4:34), and two distinct men called 'Barsabbas' (Acts 1:23; 15:22). Nevertheless, the fact remains that Bar-Jesus means 'son of Jesus', and Luke himself makes it clear that he is aware of the hidden possibilities and dangers of this name, since he has Paul begin his counter-attack in v. 10 with the address: 'You son of the devil, you enemy of all righteousness'. The one who calls himself son of Jesus reveals himself to be in fact a son of the uttermost darkness (into which he himself will soon fall), since he is fighting against the word of the Lord. Thus, we need not accept the radical supposition that Luke has deliberately invented the name 'Bar-Jesus' as an antithetical concept, since proper names such as Bar-Jesus and Barabbas are not so uncommon; at the same time, we can affirm that those who handed on Christian traditions orally and in writing were very happy to find such names in their sources, since they knew how to turn such coincidences to their own advantage.

Verse 8, where Bar-Jesus is given the new name *Elymas*, confronts us with an unsolved problem: 'Elymas the magician (for that is the meaning of his name) withstood them [i.e. Barnabas and Saul], seeking to turn away the proconsul from the faith.' The puzzle is posed by the word 'Elymas'. If we take the passage literally, we ought to understand it as a translation of 'Bar-Jesus', but this makes no sense. It has been suggested that we can discern here traces of a second, independent narrative with a sorcerer called Elymas as protagonist; Luke would have combined this with another narrative about the sorcerer Bar-Jesus, paying the price of small inconcinnities in the introduction (first it is Barnabas and Saul who find Bar-Jesus, who was in Sergius Paulus' entourage; only then are they summoned by Sergius Paulus). But the text has too little substance to permit us to dissect it into two independent units, and the problems in its introduction are due to the shortening of the perspective in the narrative. The best solution proposed hitherto seems to be the derivation of 'Elymas' from a semitic root which would roughly correspond to the Greek professional designation 'magician'; *alim*, 'wise man' in Arabic, or *haloma*, 'interpreter of dreams' in Aramaic, have been suggested. The result would be a double name like 'Simon Magus', viz. 'Bar-Jesus Elymas' or 'Bar-Jesus Magus'. While there is little evidence to support such a proposal, it is at any rate preferable to the imaginative suggestion by Theodor Zahn, which is based on the reading *Hetoimas* in Codex D. Zahn equates this Hetoimas, and hence also Bar-Jesus, with Atomos, the Jewish Cypriot magician in the text from Josephus quoted above. One could spin out a whole novel from this: thanks to Paul's intervention, Bar-Jesus loses his first patron and must look for a new job; in Josephus, we find him at a new low point in his career, because now he has to work a cheap love spell for Felix . . .[4]

b. The proconsul Sergius Paulus

In v. 7, Luke informs us that Bar-Jesus 'was with the proconsul, Sergius Paulus'. Let us begin with the strictly historical details. The island of Cyprus had been a senatorial province since 20 BCE, governed by a proconsul for one year at a time; unfortunately, we do not have a complete list of the proconsuls of Cyprus with their dates. We know of a Roman family, the Sergii Paulli (usually written in this form), who possessed estates in Pisidian Antioch. It seems that several members of this family were government officials; three inscriptions, in part very fragmentary, are usually adduced to support this claim. The most promising seems to be an inscription which mentions a Sergius Paullus as one of the inspectors

---

[4] Cf. T. Zahn, 'Zur Lebensgeschichte des Apostels Paulus', *NKZ* 15 (1904), 23–41, 189–200, see 195–200.

of the banks of the River Tiber in Rome under the emperor Claudius.[5] But nothing permits us to say with certainty that he later became proconsul on Cyprus; and even if we could ascertain this, we still would not know anything about the precise year. This is not the place to find the longed-for cornerstone for an absolutely certain Pauline chronology.

Let us return to our text. If Bar-Jesus belongs to the entourage of the proconsul Sergius Paulus, this means that he is employed as a court theologian who advises the proconsul in the various situations of life, perhaps also as a personal astrologer. There is nothing here to surprise a reader who is even slightly familiar with the classical period. Most of the Roman emperors kept their private astrologer, and they scarcely took a step without consulting him. We know the names of the most famous court astrologers, such as Thrasyllus, the counsellor of the emperor Tiberius. In his historical work, Tacitus writes about Nero's wife and about Otho, one of the unsuccessful competitors for the succession to Nero (*Hist.* 1.22, 2): 'There had been so many private astrologers—the worst kind of accoutrements in the marriage of a prince—in Poppaea's private chamber; one of them, Ptolemy, had been Otho's companion in Spain.' The examples of Otho in Spain and Felix in Judaea, in Josephus' account, show that this phenomenon could be transposed to the level of provincial governors, as we see in the case of Sergius Paulus. Most of these professional astrologers were orientals: Egyptians, Babylonians, Chaldeans, Syrians or Jews. The fact that Sergius Paulus kept a *Jewish* counsellor shows at any rate traces of an idea which we have repeatedly encountered up to this point, viz. that Judaism mediates between the Christian message and Gentiles. Sergius Paulus had already learned something from Bar-Jesus about the God of the Bible, and the Christian proclamation can build more easily on this kind of prior knowledge.

It is scarcely necessary to explain why Bar-Jesus reacts defensively when the proconsul hears the word of God from the mouths of Barnabas and Saul (v. 7) and thus comes to the Christian faith (v. 8): he sees Felix eluding his grasp, and fears losing his lucrative position. Luke attests in v. 7 that Sergius Paulus is 'a man of intelligence'. No doubt he could satisfy his curiosity for a time by paying heed to Bar-Jesus; but when something better is offered, he will appreciate its quality, and no longer let himself be taken in by the deceitful intriguing of the magician.

Let us sum up what we have ascertained thus far. The socio-cultural colouring of the entire scene fits the classical context perfectly up to this point: there was nothing exceptional in the figure of a Jewish prophet who succeeded with the help of astrology, the interpretation of dreams and other esoteric knowledge in establishing himself as court theologian to a high Roman official. Luke insults him by describing him as a magician, because he sees his Christian preachers confronted with a

---

[5] *Inscriptiones Latinae Selectae* no. 5926.

situation of acute competition. There existed a wide spectrum of religious 'special offers', often with a whiff of the exotic. The external appearance of the itinerant Christian missionaries was very similar to the 'men of God' of every shade who wandered from place to place, and they risked being evaluated against this background and absorbed into this spectrum. Great care was necessary, so that they could win through with their better message and their better miracles. Thus, our narrative is a concrete example of real situations which doubtless occurred again and again in the syncretistic Mediterranean world.

c. Saul or Paul?

It is not Barnabas, but Saul who takes on the leading role as opponent of Bar-Jesus. Here, at the beginning of v. 9, he is called Paul for the first time in the Acts of the Apostles: 'Saul, who is also called Paul.' It is here that the change of name takes place, rather than at his conversion (ch. 9, where nothing is said), although the change in his life would certainly have made this possible, from a form-critical point of view. But even here, in ch. 13, no genuine change of name occurs, even though Luke from now on consistently employs only the name Paul. 'Saulos' is the Greek form of the Hebrew name 'Saul'. The most celebrated bearer of this name was King Saul from the tribe of Benjamin, to which Paul too belonged (cf. Acts 13:21; Phil 3:5). Paul did not cease to bear this name. One reason for Luke's preference for 'Saul' up to this point is a desire to show that the future missionary to the Gentiles is rooted in Judaism. Double names were often employed in diaspora Judaism; in some cases the Roman name has nothing to do with the Hebrew name in terms of meaning, but is phonetically similar. According to Roman standards, 'Paul' (which means 'small', 'lowly') would be the third component of a full name, i.e. the cognomen. Paul probably bore this name from his childhood on. Subsequently, he employs only this name *ad extra*, in his letters.

Another factor complicating the question of names is that this change takes place precisely at the point in the narrative where Paul meets the Roman proconsul Sergius Paulus. This too has given rise to a number of hypotheses, e.g. the extreme thesis that the proconsul actually adopted the apostle. We can still find one reflection of this in the article about Sergius Paulus in a leading classical encyclopaedia, the *Kleine Pauly*, where we are told that 'the impact of meeting the proconsul led Paul to adopt his cognomen'.[6] But even this goes too far, and contradicts the better-founded supposition that Paul had a double name from his early days on.

---

[6] V. Fadinger, in KP 5, 137.

How then is this coincidence to be explained? Doubtless along the same lines as with 'Bar-Jesus': Luke has recognised and skilfully exploited the possibilities inherent in the similarity of the names. In the presence of the Roman proconsul Sergius Paulus, the career of Saul the missionary to Jews ends and the activity of Paul the missionary to Gentiles begins; his path will take him to Rome. Besides this, a change in leadership is linked with this artificial introduction of a change of name: the relationship of Barnabas and Saul is reversed, so that from now on it is Paul who sets the tone. Already here, he acts on his own, and the continuation of the journey is described in lapidary tones at v. 13: 'Now Paul and his company set sail from Paphos.'

We still have to consider the contest between Paul and Bar-Jesus. Paul is 'filled with the Holy Spirit', i.e. seized by the inspired excitement proper to a worker of miracles (v. 9). He turns a penetrating gaze on Bar-Jesus[7] and formulates a sharp invective consisting of a rhetorical question in v. 10 and the infliction of punishment in v. 11. Both parts are indebted to the Septuagint: 'Even the curses of the apostle sound a biblical note.'[8] We have already discussed the address 'son of the devil' in v. 10. Paul goes on to ask: 'Will you not stop making crooked the straight paths of the Lord?' As we recall from Lk 3:4, one who prepares the way would have the task of making a straight path for the Lord: Bar-Jesus proves to be the opposite of this, since he is blocking the path of the Lord. As a punishment, the hand of the Lord comes upon him (v. 11). The metaphor of blinding is taken literally and put into action in this passage. Bar-Jesus understood himself as a leader of the blind (Rom 2:19), one who was able to lead Gentiles along the right path. He was, however, nothing more than a blind man leading the blind, and now he is physically blinded, so that he can no longer see the sun, though only for a certain time. The threat is carried out at once, and Bar-Jesus goes about looking for people to lead him by the hand. Nevertheless, the temporal limitation leaves the conclusion open, as with Simon Magus, although we are not told anything about how Bar-Jesus reacts. His period of blindness is an opportunity for him to come to his senses: he will regain his sight, and it is to be hoped that he will then be a new man, converted.

The proconsul, who is present here and plays the part assigned to the public in miracle narratives, comes to faith in v. 12, but once again we are told explicitly the reason for this: 'He was astonished at the teaching of the Lord.' The miracle arouses astonishment, but ultimately it is the message, the gospel, the word of God (v. 7) that is decisive. In the clash of competing offers of meaning, this word proves its superiority. If we consider the passage from an historical point of view, it must be doubted

---

[7] On the verb *atenizein*, employed here and in nine other passages in Acts, cf. R. Strelan, 'Strange Stares: *Atenizein* in Acts', *NT* 41 (1999), 235–55.

[8] E. Plümacher, *Lukas als hellenistischer Schriftsteller,* 47 n. 58.

whether the proconsul did in fact accept baptism; even the article about Sergius Paulus, otherwise rather too optimistic, notes that 'one can scarcely assert that he was completely converted'.[9] Luke is enabled to show once more that even members of the upper class are interested in Christianity. No one need fear that joining the Christian community entails a loss of social position.

d. The bigger picture: (not so) hidden parallels

Great and significant beginnings are always exposed to special dangers. The opposition takes dramatic forms, as the opponents endeavour to crush the novelty in its initial stages—for otherwise it may be too late. Jesus is confronted with this kind of opposition at the start of the Gospel, in Lk 4:1–11. Three times Satan tries to get him to deviate from his path. One temptation concerns the perversion of a miracle to serve magical ends: Jesus is to change stones into bread in order to appease his hunger. Jesus emerges as the victor. Since Satan is the definitive opponent, there is no possibility of his conversion: this means that the narrative cannot have an open conclusion. When the Christian message takes a first decisive step beyond Jerusalem and reaches Samaria, the magician Simon appears at Acts 8:5–24. His idea of getting hold of the miraculous power of the Spirit by means of money represents a very grave danger to the purity of Christian teaching and praxis, but Simon Peter overcomes him. At the beginning of his missionary activity, which will go far beyond the area reached hitherto, Paul must crush a similar opposition, embodied in the person of Bar-Jesus. Both these opponents, Simon Magus and Bar-Jesus, are basically poor wretches who have been led astray, and this is why they are given the possibility of a first or renewed conversion. The fact that they involve a certain affinity to Christian themes—with Bar-Jesus it is his name, with Simon Magus his baptism—draws our attention to a depressing situation. In Luke's eyes, the greatest obstacle to the spread of the Christian message is an all-devouring syncretism which at its worst even usurps Christian substance such as the name of Jesus, and hence threatens the Church from within. This calls for resoluteness, but also for caution in dealing with believers who lapse. A final point: each time, it is the Christian proclamation that wins the trial of strength, relying not so much on a superior miraculous power, but rather on the message of salvation which it brings.

Only one other significant matter must be mentioned. Bar-Jesus is punished here by being struck blind for a certain period—precisely what had happened to Paul a short time previously. He too needed helpers to take him by the hand and lead him to Damascus (9:8). It is clear that Luke wants us to discover a hidden parallel between Paul, the itinerant

---

[9] *KP* 5, 137.

Jewish preacher and worker of miracles, and Bar-Jesus, the Jewish magician with the eloquent name, between the true prophet and the false prophet. I think that the American New Testament scholars Luke Timothy Johnson and Robert C. Tannehill are correct when they tentatively explain this as follows: 'Perhaps we are to see Saul, at the moment he takes on his new and proper identity as Paul the Apostle, fighting the final battle with the "Jewish false prophet" within him, blinding the hostile magician that is his former self at the moment he assumes his role as "light to the Gentiles" (see 13:47)'; 'Paul in denouncing Elymas is rejecting his own former personality and value structures, which remain threatening potentialities within himself.'[10] To sum up: we see Paul fighting against his own shadow, the dark parts of his own personality. He does not simply split these off and suppress them; it appears that he succeeds in integrating them.

2. In Lystra: a miracle and its consequences (Acts 14:8–20)[11]

Paul and his newly grouped missionary team now set sail for the mainland, making for Asia Minor. When they reach Perge in Pamphylia, John Mark leaves them. Luke uses the next station, Antioch in Pisidia, to introduce a great sermon by Paul which suits the occasion by containing selected portions of the Old Testament history of salvation. The double address should be noted: 'Men of Israel, and you that fear God, listen' (13:16). This is repeated later: 'Brethren, sons of the family of Abraham, and those among you that fear God' (13:26). Who are these fearers of God? Are they sympathetic Gentiles, like Cornelius in 10:1? Acts 13:43 presents some difficulties for this interpretation: here we are told that when Paul and Barnabas leave the synagogue, 'many Jews and devout converts to Judaism' follow them. 'Devout' can be understood as the equivalent of 'fearers', and the designation of these persons as proselytes would lead us once again to the pious Jews and proselytes in Acts 2:5, 11. But this uncertainty is not very significant, since the orientation to the Gentile nations emerges unmistakably a little later on in our text. Paul and Barnabas themselves proclaim at 13:46 that they will turn to the Gentiles, in keeping with the words of Isaiah: 'I have set you to be a light for the Gentiles, that you may bring salvation to the uttermost parts of the earth' (Is 48:6, quoted at Acts 13:47), and v. 48 tells us that the representative Gentiles who hear these words rejoice, praise the word of the Lord, and come to faith.

Our missionaries, driven from place to place by hostilities on the part of the local Jewish communities, arrive in v. 51 at Iconium, where they

---

[10] L. T. Johnson, *Acts*, 227; R.C. Tannehill, *Narrative Unity*, II, 163 n. 15.

[11] On this episode, cf. especially M. Fournier, *The Episode at Lystra: A Rhetorical and Semiotic Analysis of Acts 14:7–20a* (AmUSt.TR 197), New York et al. 1997; S.-Ch. Lin, *Wundertaten*, 147–287.

succeed in winning a great company of Jews and Greeks for the faith (14:1), and finally reach Lystra and Derbe, two cities of Lycaonia. The next dramatic episode is located in Lystra.

It is impossible to avoid recognising a certain logic in the development that leads from the beginning of the Acts of the Apostles to the events in Lystra. The first persons addressed by the Christian message, as witnesses of the Pentecostal event in Jerusalem, were Jews and proselytes from all the lands of the earth. These are followed by the Samaritans, who have a special (though problematic) relationship to Judaism. The next step is represented by the Ethiopian chamberlain and by the centurion Cornelius: these are nominally still Gentiles, but are scarcely distinguishable from pious Jews. Next, Paul encounters in Paphos a high Roman official, but he too has a Jewish magician in his entourage. Despite the explicit mention of the Gentile nations, the entire course of events in Pisidian Antioch is determined by the context of the Jewish synagogue. All this abruptly changes in Lystra, where no mediating Jewish influence exists. Paul and Barnabas are suddenly confronted with pure paganism and with a pure polytheistic belief which is as yet untouched by Jewish monotheism and is still far from the philosophical level of the discussion about true religion engaged in by the Epicureans and Stoics whom Paul will meet in Athens. How will these complete pagans react? How can the Christian message reach them? Where are the positive opportunities, and the dangers? These are the considerations that Luke seeks to develop, once again with the help of an impressive and detailed narrative.

In terms of literary genre, the first thing that we find in Acts 14:8–10 is a pure miracle of healing. A man lame from birth is given the power of movement by Paul; Peter had done the same in 3:1–10, and there are at least three close verbal points of contact between the two pericopae. A stable element in the narrative of a miracle is the admiring reaction of the crowd, which takes the form of an acclamation in 14:11–12. In v. 13, this reaction becomes a little event of its own, thanks to the attempt to translate this admiration into action. When the attempt is made to offer sacrifice to Paul and Barnabas, they in turn react by presenting a miniature version of their missionary sermon. The stoning of Paul follows in vv. 19–20; this may already have existed in a pre-Lukan form as a second unfriendly reaction by the frustrated crowd, as it saw that it was to be deprived of the expected sacrificial feast with plenty of meat to enjoy, but in Luke's context the stoning is provoked by hostile Jews from Pisidian Antioch.

a. The miracle

The healing miracle proper begins with a weighty description in several stages of the distress of the sick man. 'Now at Lystra there was a man sitting who (a) could not use his feet; (b) he was a cripple from birth, (c) who had never walked.' He sits there, presumably by the wayside, in order to beg enough to sustain his life. He hears Paul preach, but does not address him directly with a request for healing. All of this serves to intensify the degree of difficulty in the miracle that Paul must perform, so that we can understand the somewhat exaggerated reaction by the crowd. In addition, it is possible to read this passage as a metaphor: without help, the human person is unable to stand on his own two feet and take his path through life. Someone must take him by the arms and lift him, even if only by means of an encouraging word that shows him the path.

The very fact that Paul possesses the prophetic gift of reading hearts shows that he is a worker of miracles. He looks intently at the cripple and recognises 'that he had faith to be made well' (v. 9). On an initial level, this means that he has sufficient confidence in the worker of miracles, and that he hopes for physical healing. On a further level, it also speaks of the salvation proclaimed by the preaching of the gospel (cf. 14:7), which must be received in faith. The miraculous word, which Paul speaks with a loud voice in v. 10, has an instantaneous effect: the man springs up (confirmation) and walks around (demonstration).

b. The reaction

When this deed has been performed, the crowd begins to cry in Lycaonian, 'The gods have come down to us in the form of men!' (v. 11).[12] The Lycaonian language, remnants of which are preserved in inscriptions, has a special function here: Paul and Barnabas do indeed speak fluent Greek, but they are not so familiar with the local dialect of the populace, so that it takes them quite some time to understand what is going on. To begin with, accordingly, they show no reaction. The crowd's praise may seem a little exaggerated, when one bears in mind that the miraculous cure was after all not so very spectacular, but it is not wholly implausible. Apparitions of gods on earth in human form are a stable element of hellenistic piety—assertions to the contrary in some commentaries are nothing more than a sign that their authors have never read the 'Bible of the Greeks', Homer's epics. In the *Odyssey*, for example, the hero returns home disguised as a beggar, after long and weary wanderings. The spokesman of the suitors of Penelope, Odysseus' wife, throws a footstool at him, but the others rebuke him (17, 483–487):

> Antinoüs, you did wrong to throw that at the poor beggar. A curse on you! For gods wander even through the cities: they come in many forms, and have the appearance of strangers from a foreign country. But all the while they are testing human pride and righteousness.

[12] On what follows, cf. C. Breytenbach, 'Zeus und der lebendige Gott. Anmerkungen zur Apostelgeschichte 14.11–17', *NTS* 39 (1993), 396–413.

It would be easy to multiply examples. This brings us to the first reason why the crowd is not satisfied this time with merely identifying the presence of a numinous power in the worker of miracles (the 'divine man'), but declares that he is a god in human form. The narrator has included a second theme here. If one looks at the Gentile world of gods from the standpoint of monotheistic Judaism, one will note that the borders which it posits between god and human being are unacceptably fluid; the very fact of anthropomorphic representation, i.e. the making of statues of the gods in human form, represents a suspicious destabilisation of this distinction, and this impression is only strengthened by the idea that such gods can appear on earth. The monotheist will also note a convergence here with a tendency from the opposite direction, viz. the willingness to accord divine status to exceptional individual human beings. This presents Christian theology in a later period with problems of demarcation in the sphere of christology—what distinguishes the epiphany of such gods in human form from the incarnation of the divine Word? How is the apotheosis of divinised human beings related to the attribution to Jesus Christ of the titles 'God from God' and 'Son of God'? Answers could indeed be found; the significant point in our present context is the very fact that answers were required. For Luke and his sources, this meant that the priority was to safeguard monotheism, since this is the basis for the development of christology.

In v. 12, the two 'gods' in human form are identified. The crowd calls Barnabas Zeus: clearly, he is the older of the two and the more imposing personality in terms of his appearance. They call Paul Hermes, because he is the main speaker: one of the roles of the god Hermes in Greek mythology is to speak on behalf of Zeus and the other gods, to be their messenger and communicate their will. This is true even if there is in fact no etymological connection between the divine name 'Hermes' and the technical term 'hermeneutics', which means the theory of understanding and the art of translation. Philo of Alexandria sees such a connection on the verbal level too, when he writes in his *Legatio ad Gaium* (99):

> Hermes binds winged shoes on his feet. Why does he do this? Surely only because he must be as quick as lightning on his feet—indeed, he must fly off in urgent haste—as the interpreter and proclaimer of divine commands. It is from these tasks that he has his name.

The Jewish historian Artapanus applies the name Hermes to Moses, because he is said to have interpreted the Egyptian hieroglyphics.

This identification of Barnabas and Paul with Zeus and Hermes also serves to impart more local colouring to our narrative, and this brings us to the second reason why precisely this particular miracle of healing is followed by such a remarkable reaction. In his *Metamorphoses* (8.626–724), Ovid has preserved a saga set in Phrygia, not far from Lycaonia

and the city of Lystra. The substance of this local saga spoke of two
local gods, perhaps called Tarchunt and Runt or Pappas and Men, who
were replaced in the Greek version by Zeus and Hermes, and correspondingly in the Latin version by Jupiter and Mercury. These two wander
around in the neighbourhood like human beings. No one is willing to
show hospitality by receiving them into his house, with the exception
of the elderly couple Philemon and Baucis. They share their meagre
provisions with the gods (who are not recognised as such), and are richly
rewarded. Finally, they are even transformed into sacred trees and
venerated by their fellow-countrymen (724: 'The one whom the gods
loved is a god; let us now venerate the one who showed veneration'),
whereas retribution overtakes all the others. It is highly probable that
Luke was familiar with this saga, and that he consciously alludes to it.
He would then want us to picture the Lycaonians reacting to the miracle
by saying to one another: 'We aren't going to make the traditional mistake
again. We are not like our unhappy ancestors—we know a god when we
see one.'[13]

Gods must be venerated with sacrifices, especially in their own temple.
The priest of 'Zeus in front of the city' (a name indicating the presence
of a temple of Zeus immediately before the city gates) prepares all that
is necessary (v. 13). He brings oxen and garlands to the gate, and the
sacrificial procession is already forming, when Paul and Barnabas finally
recognise what is afoot. Now they are obliged to react, and they do so
both in deed and in word.

c. Resistance

As a prelude to the missionary sermon of Paul and Barnabas in vv. 15–
17, we are told that they tear their garments and rush in among the crowd.
The former signals their horror at the imminent blasphemy, while the
latter expresses their wish to stand on the same level as the crowd, since
they want to be reckoned among the people rather than among the gods;
besides this, gods would not behave with so little decorum. They
emphasise this also in the introductory words of their discourse, which
they apparently deliver in unison: 'Men, why are you doing this? We
also are men, of like nature with you' (v. 15a). In the Greek text, emphasis
is laid on the idea of a common capacity for suffering, which the gods
lack.

The main part of the little sermon follows in vv. 15b–17. Unlike the
lengthy address in the synagogue in Pisidian Antioch, this preaching is
addressed to Gentiles. In Luke's narrative, it serves as a forerunner to
the more detailed address on the Areopagus in ch. 17. There is no point
in further elaboration here, in a remote rural area whose populace has

[13] Cf. R. I. Pervo, *Profit with Delight*, 64f.

not yet made the acquaintance of philosophical enlightenment. For that, a better educated public is needed, and this will not be the case before Paul reaches Athens. But the motifs in 14:15–17 return in ch. 17, and provide the structure upon which the later discourse is built.

The speech begins with the admonishment in 14:15b: 'You should turn from these vain things to a living God who made the heaven and the earth and the sea and all that is in them.' This affirmation about creation takes up ideas from the Old Testament (it suffices to mention one example here, Ps 146:6), but it is impossible to overlook the connection between the demand to turn away from the useless idols and Paul's initial preaching. The apostle describes in 1 Thess 1:9 how this was received: 'You turned to God from idols, to serve a living and true God.' This similarity must be seen against the background of the proclamation of God in hellenistic diaspora Judaism: the first thing pure pagans must be told is that they are to turn away from their many idols, in order to give due honour to the one God. If they do this, they will no longer commit the error of holding mortal human beings to be gods. This determines the function of discourse about God's creative activity within the proclamation. The error of polytheism comes from venerating as gods things that are created, e.g. heavenly constellations or nature or human beings, although these are merely creatures of God.

Paul then makes a christological statement in 1 Thess 1:10: 'and to wait for his Son from heaven, whom he raised from the dead, Jesus who delivers us from the wrath to come'. This seems to come too early for Luke at this point in his narrative, where pioneer work is still to be done; nevertheless, an implicit christological horizon is hinted at. According to Acts 14:16, 'in past generations' the creator God 'allowed all the nations to walk in their own ways', and v. 17 adds that God's generosity was already at work in the pagan past of the addressees, bestowing on them rain from heaven, fruitful seasons, food and joy in their hearts. The emphasis on the element of the past implies on a subtextual level that this time of far-reaching tolerance is now over. Now it is necessary to take a new decision, in face of the new activity of the creator God in Jesus Christ.

d. Stoning

It is not at all easy for Paul and Barnabas to convince their public: 'With these words they scarcely restrained the people from offering sacrifice to them' (v. 18). It would be only logical if the crowd, frustrated of their hope of a great sacrificial meal with meat for all, now became enraged and tried to stone those who had been their heroes a short time before, and this stoning does in fact take place in v. 19—but it is carried out by Jews from Iconium. They had already tried the same thing at Iconium, but without success (14:5). Now they achieve their goal. Luke often goes beyond what his sources state, by introducing Jewish opponents as the main trouble-makers (compare e.g. 2 Cor 11:32 with Acts 9:23–25). There can be no doubt that this is a very problematic aspect of the way in which he works, and we cannot simply accept this from him without any critical objection.

Paul himself notes at 2 Cor 11:25 that he has survived a stoning. This would not have been possible in the case of a Jewish stoning, which was performed as an execution. Rather, we must assume this to be a case of lynching: an infuriated mob pursues the man, throws stones after him and achieves a direct hit so severe that he falls to the ground and either actually dies under the hail of stones or else is left lying for dead. In v. 19, the supposedly dead body of Paul is dragged out of the city, since corpses pollute the city territory; this is why burial places always lie outside the city gates. As Luke describes it in v. 20, it seems almost a miracle when Paul simply gets up again, goes into the city and leaves it for Derbe on the following morning (one might compare here Lk 4:28–30). What happens here is like a resurrection in the midst of the everyday life of the world. A little taste of resurrection is present in the tribulation experienced by a disciple of the Lord.

The narrative as a whole puts into words the tension between making contact and offering resistance. On the one hand, the Christian message must look for points of contact; it must draw attention to itself and fascinate people, and it will in fact accommodate certain expectations held by its audience, whether it wishes to do so or not. On the other hand, this immediately generates the risk that it will be absorbed into already-existing patterns and categories of thought; at worst, this would lead to a fundamental distortion and falsification of the message. Here, the Christian proclamation has an 'educational task' to carry out. One can define this more precisely as a 'commission to engage in the critique of religion': 'It is necessary to elaborate in specific terms the salvific consequences of the distinction that the theology of creation posits between God and the world (the human person) . . . The work of theological enlightenment proves fundamentally to be a work of correction: there are no gods in human form . . .'[14]

---

[14] R. Pesch, *Apg*, 60.

V

PAUL IN GREECE (ACTS 16–18)

1. An 'exorcism' in Philippi (Acts 16:16–24)

After the apostolic council, Paul sets out with Silas at Acts 15:40 on his second great missionary journey, which takes in Greece and ends at 19:1–20 in Ephesus. This is followed by the programmatic double verse (19:21f.) which begins the journey to Jerusalem—a journey of farewell, since it leads Paul into Roman captivity. Paul makes great haste through Asia Minor. In Troas on the western coast, a man from Macedonia appears to Paul in a vision by night, urging him to cross over and help them (16:9), and Paul is at once persuaded. The first city on the European mainland he reaches, via the island of Samothrace and the port of Neapolis, is Philippi. The 'we'-form, which appears for the first time within the text of Acts at 16:10 ('. . . immediately we sought to go on into Macedonia, concluding that God had called us to preach the gospel to them'), and then suddenly disappears from the narrative of this episode at 16:17 (the soothsaying slave-girl 'followed Paul and us'), indicates that he is not alone. It is probably Luke himself who has imprinted this 'we'-form on specific textual material, either in order to introduce himself as an eyewitness or else to signalise that he is drawing on material from the group of Paul's companions, e.g. from Silas. At any rate, his intention is to strengthen the impression of credibility in his narratives.[1]

a. The city of Philippi[2]

Philippi lies on the Via Egnatia, the main road link between east (Asia Minor) and west (Italy and Rome), about 15 kilometres inland from the coast and the port. It bears the name of Philip II, king of Macedonia and father of Alexander the Great. According to Acts 16:11, Philippi was a Roman colony at the time of Paul; the history behind this is as follows. The decisive battle between Brutus and Cassius, who had murdered

[1] Cf. J. Wehnert, *Die Wir-Passagen der Apostelgeschichte. Ein lukanisches Stilmittel aus jüdischer Tradition* (GTA 40), Göttingen 1989.

[2] On Philippi, cf. P. Pilhofer, *Philippi*, I: *Die erste christliche Gemeinde Europas* (WUNT 97), Tübingen 1995; II: *Katalog der Inschriften von Philippi* (WUNT 119), Tübingen 2000; L. Bormann, *Philippi. Stadt und Christengemeinde zur Zeit des Paulus* (NT.S 78), Leiden 1995.

Caesar, and the triumvirs Octavian (later the emperor Augustus) and Mark Antony had taken place near the city. In the aftermath, Mark Antony distributed land here to the veterans of his army (42 BCE). Augustus, who settled citizens from Italy in Philippi in 31/30 BCE, is considered the real founder of the city, and this is why the city had a Roman administration, headed by Roman officials. It was freed from a number of fiscal obligations, and its Roman inhabitants were treated on the same basis as the inhabitants of Italian cities. This had profound consequences for their mental attitudes; far away from the centre, they defended their own Roman identity with unmistakable pride. This could, however, be exaggerated and turn into xenophobia, i.e. hostility to everything that seemed foreign.

As might be expected, excavations in Philippi have disclosed more Latin than Greek inscriptions. In religious terms, archaeological evidence (temples, statues, inscriptions, coins) reveals the coexistence of various forms of religion. The worship of the ancient Greek deities was not strongly represented, whereas new imports from the east, especially from Egypt, gradually established themselves. Above all, however, Roman deities were known and worshipped, and the imperial cult was also practised. Our other sources are silent about the presence of Jews among the inhabitants of the city. They cannot have been very numerous, but their existence is presupposed when Paul visits a place of prayer outside the city gates beside a river, on the sabbath day (16:13), and repeats this visit during the following days (16:16). In Greek, this place of prayer is called *proseukhê*, a technical term in the Jewish diaspora for the synagogue building. The localisation near water, attested many times, was intended to make it easier to perform the prescribed ritual washings. In the case of Philippi, one may also wonder whether a site outside the city points to a certain hostility to foreigners which made it impossible to find a location inside the city, although legal prohibitions in this sense are unknown.

One Roman author describes such colonies in general terms as 'a kind of copy and sketch of the city of Rome in miniature'.[3] This automatically prompts the question whether Luke already envisages the final goal of the narrative, namely Rome, when the first thing Paul does on Greek soil is to enter a Roman colony. We can infer from the Letter to the Philippians that he did in fact found the community in Philippi and that he always prized it, looking on it as his favourite community. According to Luke, the local community in Philippi began in the house of a woman called Lydia, a seller of purple from Thyateira (16:14). Paul encounters her in a group of women at the place of prayer, so it is permissible to infer her status as a God-fearer (v. 14 calls her 'a worshipper

---

[3] Aulus Gellius, *Attic Nights*, 16.13, 9.

of God'). She and her whole household are baptised; it is clear that she is the head of the house. She prevails upon the Christian missionaries to stay with her (16:15), and when they have been set free from prison they return to her house, where they speak once again with the sisters and brothers before taking their leave (16:40). Like the household of Cornelius in Caesarea, the household of Lydia in Philippi proves its worth as the centre of the growing community.

b. The slave-girl who was a soothsayer

We must however begin by looking at the soothsaying slave-girl and her confrontation with Paul. In terms of genre, this text is an exorcism cast in a very remarkable form; it is the first, but not the last exorcism in the Acts of the Apostles (cf. 19:13–16). We are told in 16:16 that the female protagonist was a young slave who had 'masters'. This means that she belonged to two or more owners, who may have been a married couple, a consortium of heirs, or even a business consortium. The logion of Jesus to the effect that 'no slave can serve two masters' (Lk 16:13) may occur to us here; but such a situation was in fact rather frequent, even if it was not the rule. The theme of Cicero's plea on behalf of the actor Quintus Roscius is the rights in one slave shared by two owners who have become enemies. In such a case, profits and expenses were shared—the profits that the slave earned through his or her work, and the costs incurred in keeping the slave alive.

We are then told that the slave-girl 'had a spirit, Python'. The proper name of the spirit is connected with the slave-girl's activity, her 'soothsaying' mentioned at the close of v. 16. In Greek mythology, the name 'Pytho(n)' belonged to a great snake, like a dragon, that guarded a shaft in the earth in Delphi. When the god Apollo reached Delphi in the course of his wanderings, he liked the place so much that he wanted to settle there. Since, however, the snake was unwilling to leave the place, he had first to defeat it in a battle. From then on, the name 'Python' was attributed to the god himself. According to the myth, he founded the oracular site in Delphi which was to develop into the most celebrated oracular sanctuary in the classical world. A woman from Delphi was used as seer; at peak periods of popularity, several women were employed. After preparatory ceremonies, she descended into a secret room on a deeper level within the temple of Apollo, where the spirit took hold of her and she delivered answers to the enquiries addressed to the oracle by word of mouth or in writing. Her name was 'Pythia', whereas 'Python' can also denote a common ventriloquist who worked by means of various tricks. It appears that many people attempted to use this model to explain how the Pythia spoke with 'a voice not her own', but Plutarch angrily dismisses this as a misunderstanding of what happens when an oracle is delivered:

For it is simple-minded, indeed childish to believe that the god himself, like those ventriloquists who now go by the name of 'Python', enters the bodies of the prophets and speaks from within them, employing their mouth and tongue as his instrument.[4]

This passage informs us *inter alia* that oracular priests and priestesses were also called prophets among the Greeks. We may leave open here the question whether the slave-girl in Philippi had mastered the technique of ventriloquism and made an impression in this way, or whether she worked in a different manner; it is at any rate clear that we are here in the realm of the classical *manteia*, a concept which embraces the art of soothsaying and everything connected with oracles. Although the Old Testament is familiar with certain kinds of oracles obtained by casting lots, oracular vocabulary appears in the Septuagint almost exclusively with a negative slant. A great distance is posited between the genuine prophets and the givers of oracles; it is lying prophets, unreliable interpreters of signs and of dreams, and those who summon up the dead that are linked with the oracles. A classical example is King Saul's visit to the 'witch' of Endor. The Septuagint says once that the seer engages in 'soothsaying' and three times that she engages in 'ventriloquism' (1 Sam 28:6–9).

Another important element in Luke's description of the slave-girl is a specifically Jewish Christian perspective. Greek theories of inspiration reckon with a genuine ecstasy on the part of the seer, who is flooded by the *pneuma* for a time, but they do not know of a genuine possession. Here, however, the soothsaying slave-girl, in analogy to the Gospel narratives of exorcism, counts as possessed—not indeed immediately by a demonic, evil or impure spirit, but by a spirit with the eloquent name 'Python'. This also makes it possible to 'treat' her by employing the familiar techniques of the exorcist.

Verse 16 also tells us that her owners had 'much gain' from the soothsaying slave-girl; it was, therefore, in their interest that she should function as well as possible. We can picture the scene: they have positioned their slave-girl in the market place, so that anyone who wishes can come up to her, pay a sum of money, then fire off his question in the hope of an answer. Thus, there is a great social gulf between what went on here and what went on at Delphi. In the classical period, kings and city states sent their delegations with rich presents to the sanctuary and formulated enquiries dealing with matters of high political significance; this was not seldom a question of war and peace. Plutarch complains that in his own period, at the turn of the first and second centuries CE, the Delphic oracle had fallen into general decline, but even if no longer so much frequented, it remained rooted in its locality, continued to function, and enjoyed some respect. This decline was not least due to the cheap offers available

---

[4] Plutarch, *De defectu oraculorum* ('On the Decline of Oracles'), 9 (441e).

everywhere, with a scaled-down Pythia and organisers who were perhaps not much more than itinerant mountebanks; this combination of religion and commerce, which had already proved successful in the case of Delphi, functioned well in such cases as the slave-girl in Philippi too. Faced with an uncertain future that evoked anxiety, and confronted with difficult personal decisions, people continued to find refuge in the oracles, and they were also willing to pay for this help in taking decisions. Fragments of an ancient oracle book show the kinds of questions that were posed. These are sometimes very banal:

Will I receive my wages?
Will I remain in the place to which I am now going?
Will I be sold (as a slave)?
Will my friend bring me any gain?
Will I be transferred to the heirs (of my master)?
Will I get a holiday?
Will I receive the money?
Will I be successful?
Ought I to run away?
Will they catch me, if I run away?
Will I be divorced from my wife?
Have I been poisoned?
Will I receive a bequest?[5]

c. Paul as 'exorcist'[6]

Verse 17 relates that the slave-girl runs after Paul and his group and cries at the top of her voice, 'These men are servants of the highest God, who proclaim to you the way of salvation.' When Luke tells us that she 'cries loudly', he means us to understand these words, which sound like a confession of faith or an acclamation, as an affirmation inspired by the soothsaying spirit. At first sight, they appear remarkably correct, and one would suppose that they match the self-understanding of the Christian messengers as servants of the one God and proclaimers of his words; this makes it difficult to understand why Paul reacts so negatively in v. 18. Let us then look more closely at the girl's words.

---

[5] Papyrus Oxyrhynchus XII no. 1477, 72–92 (excerpts). See J. Hengstl, *Griechische Papyri aus Ägypten als Zeugnisse des öffentlichen und privaten Lebens* (TuscBü), Munich 1978, 162f.; A. S. Hunt and C. C. Edgar, *Select Papyri*, I (LCL 266), Cambridge, Mass. and London 1932, reprint 1988, 436–9.

[6] On what follows, cf. P. R. Trebilco, 'Paul and Silas, 'Servants of the Most High God' (Acts 16.16–18)', *JSNT* 36 (1989), 51–73; and most recently also F. S. Spencer, 'Out of Mind, out of Voice: Slave-girls and Prophetic Daughters in Luke–Acts', *Biblical Interpretation* 7 (1999), 133–55; C. S. de Vos, 'Finding a Charge that Fits: The Accusation against Paul and Silas at Philippi (Acts 16.19–21)', *JSNT* 74 (1999), 51–63.

We find a first clue in the divine predicate 'the highest'. The Greek Bible has no hesitation in using it more than 110 times, clearly no longer aware of what 'the Highest' actually implies, viz. that there exist other gods too—an entire pantheon, with God's role merely that of presiding over them all. In a somewhat blurred sense, this title was taken as a general designation of God's sovereignty over human beings, the world and the angelic beings (behind whom there might lurk gods who had lost their divinity). In the intertestamental literature, however, and in Jewish inscriptions this divine predicate is found less frequently, and Philo and Josephus display a significant reserve in regard to it. We must make a further distinction between the isolated term 'the Highest' and the attributive use in the phrase 'the highest God'. Luke copies biblical language by writing rather often of 'the Highest', but he speaks only in one other passage of the highest God. The demonic throng who speak to Jesus on pagan territory through the mouth of one possessed call him 'Son of the highest God' (Lk 8:28; Mk 5:7). Besides this, predicates such as *Zeus Hypsistos* ('the highest Zeus') or *Theos Hypsistos* ('the highest god') are known from the non-Jewish world. Obviously, both Jews and early Christians were increasingly aware of the danger of the undesirable Gentile connotations which made the 'highest God' merely one among many.

Verse 17 describes the content of the missionary preaching as 'the way of salvation'. We have already said something about the motif of the 'way', when discussing Bar-Jesus' attempt to 'make crooked the straight paths of the Lord' (13:10). Let us add here that Acts can also give Christianity the simple name 'the way': Saul travels to Damascus as a persecutor of the Christians, in order to see 'whether he might find any there belonging to the way' (9:2; cf. 24:14, 22). A path is offered, along which people can enter true life. Being en route to a goal becomes a distinguishing mark of the Christian existence. But the slave-girl's words have no article before the noun, so that one could also translate: 'they proclaim to you *a* way of salvation', implying that the Christian path is only one among many. This means that it is no longer so clear that the path to salvation is involved—and *sōtēria*, 'salvation', was itself also a salvific promise of the ancient mystery cults, while *sōtēr*, 'redeemer', was a title shared by the saviour god Asclepius, the divinised emperor, and many others.

We see, therefore, that the affirmation of the slave-girl is more ambiguous than might be desired. It is possible to read her words in a perfectly correct manner: when she speaks of the highest God, she means the creator God of the Bible, and when she speaks of the way of salvation, she means the soteriological efficacy of the gospel message. But a syncretistic misunderstanding would be equally possible: a new higher god is announced, a competitor to those who already exist, and a new offer of salvation with a new redeemer-figure aims merely at widening the existing spectrum, without being fundamentally different from other offers. It is surely not without reason that the word in Greek for 'proclaiming' here is not (as so frequently) *euangelizesthai*, but the more neutral *katangellein*, employed by the Greeks when announcing the sacred feasts of their gods.

The slave-girl continues her strange activity of running after the missionaries and crying aloud for many days, until Paul finally loses patience and takes action (v. 18). Scholars have always found his long delay here problematic, and various attempts at an explanation have been proposed; for example, that Paul found the sheer volume of noise intolerable in the long term (surely an excessively banal solution), or that Paul did not require this kind of support—the demons in the gospel likewise confess Jesus to be the Son of God in words that are partly correct from a formal point of view, but they are condemned to silence, because such a confession would lose its value if it came from their mouth. This is true, but it does not account for the time factor. If we take our starting point in the fundamental ambiguity of what the slave-girl professes, we can make sense of the delay as follows: Paul ought in principle to have protested immediately, in order to ward off misunderstandings, but he did not do so, since he foresaw and feared the negative consequences (which were subsequently realised). However, the continuous repetition without clearer specification made the public formula more and more problematic, especially since there were an increasing number of new converts and these took exception to it. Not the least reason for their irritation was that Paul not only let a soothsayer go about her business unhindered, but even seemed to welcome her support. Was it possible for her to continue to provide her consultations under the cloak of Christianity? And would that mean that the Christian faith was compatible with the practice of oracles? The borders begin to be fluid, the clear contours begin to be lost to sight. This is why Paul is now compelled to shoulder the risk of silencing the spirit that speaks out of the slave-girl.

It proves very simple to overcome the soothsaying spirit by means of a command to depart from her (modelled on the exorcisms). Paul turns to the slave-girl and addresses the spirit directly: 'I charge you in the name of Jesus Christ to come out of her.' By introducing the name of Jesus Christ, Paul also makes unambiguous the references to the highest God and the way of salvation (v. 17): the highest God is the God and Father whom Jesus himself proclaimed, and the way of salvation is the way that John the Baptist made level for him, the path on which human beings are to follow him. In v. 18 a statement of confirmation concludes the miracle story: the spirit departed from the slave-girl 'that very hour'. This confirmation is skilfully picked up and developed in v. 19: 'When her owners saw that their hope of gain was gone', they too reacted. Strictly speaking, it is the soothsaying spirit that has gone out of the slave-girl, but it was only with the help of this spirit that her owners could use her to make money. Thus it is not without reason that they see the departure of the spirit as the departure of every future possibility of making profit.

d. Hostile reactions

This brings us to the hostile reactions to the miracle. The slave-girl's owners feel that Paul has damaged them, since he has seized their property and rendered it useless. In the following passage, however, they do not say this: they do not accuse Paul of damaging their property, but put forward other reasons as a pretext. This unmasks them as the real evil-doers in this narrative. Like Simon Magus, they link faith and business. Their only motive for what they do is the desire for profit; they exploit a helpless slave-girl, deceive people who are looking for help, and finally exact their revenge by bringing Paul and Silas into grave danger through bare-faced lies and clever manipulation.

The next passage shows us something more of the political circumstances in a Roman colony. The slave-girl's owners succeed in bringing Paul and Silas to the forum, before the city authorities. There are two chief officials, in Latin called *duumviri*; our text calls them *stratēgoi* (v. 20). It was their duty to maintain calm and good order.

We must look more closely at the accusation that the masters of the slave-girl bring against Paul and Silas in vv. 20f.: these men are *Jews* who are sowing confusion in the city, because they introduce '*customs* which it is not lawful for us *Romans* to accept or practise'. Thus, Paul and his companion are not identified as Christians, but as Jews. This is not so surprising, when we bear in mind that it was only a short while before that outsiders in Antioch had begun to notice a distinction and to speak of 'Christians' (Acts 11:26). The disturbing customs mentioned in the accusation refer to particularities of Judaism such as circumcision, the sabbath observance and dietary prescriptions. Here, these things are not attributed to a law, but are called an ethos, i.e. a specific code of conduct. This is in keeping with a perception *ab extra* which classifies Judaism as a cultural phenomenon, rather than taking it seriously in terms of belief, in keeping with its own self-understanding, and the result is that Jewish convictions become the antithesis of the *mos maiorum*, the good old customs of one's ancestors. A Roman who threw these customs overboard would be abandoning his own identity, and anyone who put them at risk must reckon with the charge of sowing confusion.

Naturally, Paul and Silas had not in fact proclaimed Jewish customs; but it is precisely here that the manipulation exists on the narrative level. The slave-girl's owners appeal to the pride of the colonists in their Roman identity. They exploit xenophobia and awaken the latent antisemitism which repeatedly attacked Judaism for its refusal to let itself be assimilated and integrated. On the higher, textual-pragmatic level, Luke lets the reader understand that the accusations made here cannot apply to Christianity. First of all, Christianity is not mentioned in direct speech, so that the accusations concern only Judaism (if at all); and secondly, Luke creates a distance not only between Christianity and Jewish customs, but also between Christianity and the very concept of 'ethos', which was applied to foreign peoples and their religions. He sees Christianity as the 'way' (cf. Acts 9:2; 24:22, etc.): this is to be understood as a fundamental attitude to life, rather than as something made concrete in particular (and sometimes rather remarkable) rules of conduct. The philosophical schools too tend to use 'way' more in this sense.

The accusers win over the crowd, so that the chief officials can no longer dismiss the matter as trivial. They are obliged to act, and they order Paul and Silas to be beaten and thrown into prison (vv. 22f.). Here, once again, we have the possibility of checking what Luke says: at 2 Cor 11:25, Paul affirms that he has three times been beaten with rods, and this can refer only to the Roman punishment of beating, not to the Jewish flogging which he mentions at 11:24. At 1 Thess 2:2, he recalls how he had suffered and been ill-treated at Philippi before he arrived in Thessalonica.

This could be the end of the story, since this punishment suffices for such a harmless case. The delinquents could be released on the following morning and sent away (cf. Acts 16:35). But at this point Luke inserts a second, independent episode, which is prepared at vv. 23f. The officials make the jailer personally responsible for ensuring that Paul and Silas are 'kept safely', and he promptly throws them into the innermost dungeon and fastens their feet in stocks. About midnight, while Paul and Silas are singing and praying, an earthquake shakes the foundations of the prison, all the doors are opened and the fetters are unfastened (vv. 25f.). The jailer is about to kill himself with his sword, since he assumes that the prisoners have flown (v. 27), but Paul speaks up and tells him that all are still there (v. 28). On hearing this—and once again this is significant for our subject—the jailer falls down before Paul and Silas (v. 29) and addresses them: 'My lords, what must I do to be saved?' (v. 30). They reply, 'Believe in the Lord Jesus, and you will be saved, you and your household' (v. 31). We note the contrast between the jailer on the one hand, who falls down before Paul and Silas and calls them 'lords', and their reference to 'the Lord Jesus' on the other hand, which recalls Peter's rejection of Cornelius' *proskynēsis* at 10:25f. Even to be addressed as 'lords' (*kyrioi*) is too much for Christian preachers, since there is only one *Kyrios*, Jesus Christ, and their whole existence is orientated towards him.

The baptism of the jailer and his family (v. 33), which follows immediately, adds a new family to the community in Philippi. At vv. 37–39, Paul plays the card of his Roman citizenship, a little late perhaps, but effectively. In terms of the psychology of the narrative, this is intended to salvage the honour of Christianity by showing that it does not spread any foreign, un-Roman customs.

e. Retrospect and prospect

Every new step entails dangers of its own. As in Samaria and on Cyprus, this time too the missionaries are confronted with a religious phenomenon that derives from the popular sphere of magic, astrology and soothsaying. This must be overcome, if the purity and clarity of the Christian message are not to be imperilled in the long run.

This time, however, the opposition seems very reduced, if we look only at the person of the soothsaying slave-girl, since it is also possible to attribute a correct Christian sense to her acclamation, which sounds like a confession of faith. In this case, we would have here a classic case of foreign prophecy: in the Old Testament, non-Jews like Balaam could also make accurate prophetical utterances, and here one might find something useful even in the Gentile art of soothsaying, or at least in the persons who practise it. Nevertheless, we must reaffirm the ambiguity of the oracular utterance of the slave-girl, and it remains necessary to explain why Paul exorcises the soothsaying spirit. If one emphasises this point, the text demonstrates that Christians have other options than consulting pagan soothsayers and interpreters of the future, since these persons are clearly inferior.

There is another reason for the obvious reserve in the way in which the slave-girl is dealt with: Luke describes her as a pathetic specimen of humanity. She has been deprived of her freedom and must work as a fairground attraction, practising her arts for tiny wages. One cannot judge her and condemn her for this; rather, the reader's anger is directed exclusively to her owners. Luke succeeds in denouncing the way in which a poor girl is exploited by heartless owners who are interested only in their own profit.

But what happens to the slave-girl, when our text removes her from the stage? We are often told that the exorcism of the soothsaying spirit meant that she was given her freedom, but this is unsatisfactory, as Ivoni Richter Reimer has correctly demonstrated in her book.[7] Hitherto, she was a valuable slave who earned money for her owners, so that they were concerned about her well-being; now she is still a slave, but she has become useless to her owners, and this will certainly not improve her situation.

---

[7] Cf. I. Richter Reimer, *Frauen in der Apostelgeschichte des Lukas. Eine feministisch-theologische Exegese*, Gütersloh 1992, esp. 91–161 (on Lydia), 162–201 (on the slave-girl); Eng. tr. by L. M. Maloney, *Women in the Acts of the Apostles: A Feminist Liberation Perspective*, Minneapolis 1995.

This is where Ivoni Richter Reimer begins her reflections. A consideration of the general historical background and other factors lead her to make a connection between Lydia and the slave-girl via the Jewish place of prayer. We have inscriptions, some of Jewish origin and some Gentile, which contain a dedication to the highest God and mention a *proseukhē*. These served as documents for the manumission of male and female slaves, whose Gentile masters freed them through the agency of the synagogue community, which either acted as patron or else formally took charge of the slaves. This represents a possible legal model for Lydia and the other women attached to the *proseukhē* in Philippi. They had witnessed the whole story, and they must have been concerned about what would happen to the poor slave-girl. They would have been able to persuade her Gentile masters (perhaps by paying the sum required) to set her free and hand her over to the Christian community, where she can now live as a free woman among free persons, a Christian woman among Christian sisters and brothers (v. 40).

This 'happy ending' does justice to all social, pastoral and feminist concerns. It recognises a painful gap in the narrative and adduces further material to help close it. The question does however remain whether the text itself really suggests such a solution. Is not this proposal rather the work of creative imagination, elaborating on loose threads of the narrative?

2. *Visiting Athens (Acts 17:16–21, 32–34)*[8]

From Philippi, the little missionary team takes the road southwards, via Amphipolis and Apollonia, until they reach the city of Thessalonica (Acts 17:1), where they again succeed in founding a community. The usual wrangles occur, once again at the instigation of the Jews. The accusations levelled in their absence against Paul and his companions before the city prefect amount to conspiracy against Rome: 'These men who have turned the world upside down . . . are all acting against the decrees of Caesar, saying that there is another king, Jesus' (17:6f.). Paul had in fact said only that Jesus was the Messiah awaited by the Jewish people (17:3). The translation of this matter of faith into political discourse has no more substance than any of the accusations made against Paul; but this is something we have known at least since Philippi. Nevertheless, this conflict compels them to take flight and find refuge in Beroea (17:10), where Silas and Timothy remain behind (17:14). The disturbances at Thessalonica are exported to Beroea also (17:13), so that Paul is brought to Athens (17:15). His travelling companions leave him and bring Silas

---

[8] For an overview of Acts 17:16–34 (Paul in Athens, with the Areopagus speech), see (with up-to-date bibliography) C. K. Barrett, *Acts*, II, 822–55; B. Witherington, *Acts*, 511–35; J. A. Fitzmyer, *Acts*, 599–617; C. W. Stentschke, *Luke's Portrait of Gentiles*, 203–24.

and Timothy instructions to set out for Athens as quickly as possible. It is, however, only in Corinth that they catch up with Paul (18:5). This means that Paul is completely alone in the decisive confrontation with paganism in Athens, the stronghold of non-Christian thought.

Paul himself writes in his First Letter to the Thessalonians that he longs to visit the community, and has often made plans to do so, but that this is simply impossible (1 Thess 2:17f.). When this interruption of his contact with the community becomes intolerable, he resolves, as a minimum measure, to send Timothy in his place, and he is willing to pay the price of remaining in Athens alone: 'When we could bear it no longer, we were willing to be left behind at Athens alone, and we sent Timothy, our brother and God's servant in the gospel of Christ, to establish you in your faith and to exhort you' (1 Thess 3:1f.). Paul's words diverge from Luke's account by indicating that Timothy initially stayed with him in Athens, but they do at any rate give striking confirmation both that Paul was in Athens and that he was alone for a period.

In another point too, Luke's picture corresponds to what we find in Paul's letters: despite individual conversions mentioned by Luke, no local community was founded in Athens. No letter from Paul to Athens exists, nor does he mention the city again; none of Paul's collaborators comes from Athens. There is no reference to Attica and Athens when Paul speaks about the collection—a topic occupying a great deal of space in the Corinthian correspondence. We can only surmise the reason for this relative failure. Perhaps the fact that Paul's well-tried collaborators were not with him played a role; perhaps also the fact that there were few Jews in Athens (unlike Corinth, cf. Acts 18:2–4), so that there was no milieu of 'God-fearers'. We should also bear in mind two factors to which we shall return below, viz. the small size of the population and their particular mentality.

Thus we have agreement on the most important fundamental data. Yet Luke had only a few notes for his artistic construction, mainly stations on the itinerary linked to personal names such as those of Dionysius and Damaris at Acts 17:34, and other scanty pieces of information. He could also fall back on traditional motifs and his cultural general knowledge. One example of a traditional element is found in the Areopagus discourse, which presents a basic concern already seen in the missionary preaching to Gentiles in Lystra (14:15–17): the proclamation of monotheism and of faith in God as Creator. With the aid of his cultural knowledge, Luke creates before our inner eye a vivid, distinctive picture of the city of Athens within his narrative framework.

a. Taking a look at the city

Ernst Haenchen remarks pointedly about Athens in the first century of the Common Era that it was 'a quiet little town of about 5,000 inhabitants, living off its great past'.[9] The figure of 5,000 includes only free citizens with voting rights, amounting to c.20% of the population, which thus was about five times more numerous. Even so, Athens lies far behind Corinth, which is estimated to have had about 100,000 inhabitants. It was only in the second century that Athens experienced growth, under the Roman Antonine emperors. Nevertheless, the name of the city had a special ring even in the days of Paul and Luke because of its exceptional past, with an incomparable cluster of poets and thinkers. The philosophical schools continued their work to a certain extent in Athens. Illustrious religious festivals were celebrated, drawing visitors from distant places, e.g. those who sought initiation into the mysteries of Eleusis (near Athens). The Romans made Athens the goal of what we must call an educational tourism. In one of his discourses, Cicero calls Athens the city 'whence derive education and science, belief in the gods and agriculture, justice and law', a city 'so highly respected that the faded name of Greece, now well nigh extinguished, is held aloft only by the fame of Athens'.[10]

The narrative framework begins at v. 16 with a structural element beloved in classical travel accounts, known as *periēgēsis*—a foreigner enters a city or a sanctuary and wanders around looking at statues, altars and images. He asks passers-by what these mean, providing an opportunity to insert anecdotes and excursus. This motif is clearly introduced in the opening of the Areopagus discourse: 'For as I passed along, and observed the objects of your worship . . .' (v. 23). It is indicated in v. 16 when Luke notes that Paul was filled with fury when he 'saw that the city was full of idols'.

Every map of classical Athens, with the Agora and the Acropolis, shows us the temples and other buildings that Paul could have seen. For example, the temples of Aphrodite, of Hephaistos, of Apollo and of Ares are grouped around the Agora, as well as a shrine of Zeus, an altar consecrated to twelve gods and a shrine of herms. This last edifice may have provoked particular disgust in Paul, since such herms were nothing other than cultic stones with a bearded head and an erect phallus. But it would be imprudent and dangerous for Paul to ventilate his rage by destroying the nearest stones he finds. In his speech, he employs a delicate reserve when speaking about this matter, not without a touch of irony.

More neutral observers confirm that there were very many cultic edifices and objects in Athens and attest that the Athenians were especially pious (cf. v. 22). This is however evaluated polemically in v. 16, from a Jewish perspective. The word for 'idol', *eidōlon*, was not normally employed by the Greeks for their statues of the gods and votive gifts. In classical usage it already denotes a lack of genuine existence, since it is

---

[9] E. Haenchen, *Apg*, 496. At 498 n. 7 he compares the city in the classical period to the 'old town in Heidelberg' today.

[10] Cicero, *Pro Flacco* ('On behalf of Flaccus'), 62.

employed for lifeless souls, for shadowy and deceptive images; the Septuagint and diaspora Judaism adapted it not only to designate the gods and their images in the Gentile world that surrounded them, but also to attack these as pagan idols.

b. Recollections of Socrates

The familiar pattern of proclamation—first to the Jews in the synagogue, then to the Gentiles—is varied slightly in v. 17. Paul seems to engage for a certain period both in discussions with Jews and God-fearers in the synagogue, especially on the sabbath, and in his daily activity in the market-place where he speaks to everyone who happens to pass by and meet him. This last observation by Luke not only indicates a fundamental missionary openness, no longer needing rejection by Judaism as a force which impels it outwards, but also brings into view behind the figure of Paul the shadow of one of the great men of Athenian intellectual history: Socrates. It was precisely by speaking to everyone in the market-place that Socrates irritated the Athenians. It was no longer possible to stroll calmly across the Agora—there was a risk that Socrates would take one by the sleeve at any moment and involve one by means of an apparently harmless question ('Where are you rushing off to?') in a discussion about the meaning of life, as happened to Socrates' pupil Xenophon.

The reminiscences of Socrates are continued in the next verses. In v. 18, some people take Paul for 'a preacher of foreign divinities', a main point in the accusation at Socrates' trial: 'Socrates does evil, for he does not acknowledge the gods whom the state acknowledges, while introducing other, novel divine beings.'[11] As Paul debated with the philosophers, so Socrates debated with the sophists. Socrates was brought to court, Paul was brought before the Areopagus, and like Socrates in his *Apologia*, he begins his Areopagus discourse with the address: 'Men of Athens'. This is, however, the final parallel, since there is neither trial nor condemnation of Paul. But these allusions do much to create a correct local Athenian atmosphere, and they place the apostle in a particular light. Within the framework of biblical thinking, affirmations about the Servant of the Lord are transferred to Paul; the same effect is achieved in a purely Greek context by connecting him to Socrates.

c. Epicureans and Stoics

As he takes his place day by day in the Agora, Paul also encounters the members of the philosophical schools who had their teaching institutes in Athens, and these look on him with suspicion. This is the decisive difference between the Areopagus discourse and the situation in Lystra:

[11] Xenophon, *Memorabilia* ('Recollections of Socrates') 1.1, 1.

Paul is no longer dealing with an unenlightened provincial crowd, but with an educated city public. No priest stands ready to offer sacrifice to the gods in human form; instead, we find representatives of an intellectual criticism of religion with which Christian theology can agree up to a point. Luke exploits this constellation to the full in Paul's discourse, where he makes a temporary pact with philosophy against polytheism until he reveals where the boundaries of philosophy lie and where it does not go far enough in its endeavour to arrive at a concept of God.

According to v. 18, these philosophers can be defined more precisely as Epicureans and Stoics. What are the characteristics of these two groups? And why are only these two named, and not (for example) the Academicians from the school of Plato, the Peripatetics who maintained the inheritance of Aristotle, the Sceptics and the Neopythagoreans? The second question is easier to answer: at that period, the Epicureans and the Stoics enjoyed the widest influence, and they specialised in an activity that one could call in modern language pastoral care, life counselling or psychotherapy. They took care of the individual human being and aimed to help him succeed in life. Their programme was *eudaimonia*, 'happiness'. Apart from this, other pastoral institutions did not exist in the Graeco-Roman world; the priests in the temples were not in the least concerned with this. Thus the philosophical schools, with their practical orientation, were the only serious rivals to Christianity in this field.

Epicurus, the founder of the Epicurean school, had many fervent admirers in antiquity, but in general he had acquired the bad name of an atheist and libertine, thanks to a distorted account of his teaching about the gods and his pleasure principle. He avowed that he did not uphold atheism. Nevertheless, he banished the gods to distant intermediary worlds where they led their blissful life untouched by events on earth, hence untouched also by prayers and sacrifices. Epicurus did in fact elevate to a programme the principle that one should always and in all circumstances seek pleasure and avoid pain, but if we look more closely, we discover that his basic intention was to cope with human life, shot through as it is by painful experiences, without abandoning oneself to illusions and deceitful hopes. His practical counsels tend towards an ascetic lifestyle, and differ in practice scarcely at all from the recommendations of the Stoa. But Luke will certainly not have made such fine distinctions in his evaluation of Epicureanism. Rather, he followed the customary stereotypes, which are summarised with self-irony by the Roman poet Horace, an adherent of Epicurus: 'And if you want a good laugh, then come and visit me. You will find me stout and comfortable, my body well looked after, a real little swine out of Epicurus' herd.'[12] Horace himself did not mean these words altogether seriously, but Luke would have found them a true portrait of Epicureanism.

[12] Horace, *Ep.* ('Letters') 1.4, 15f.

The Stoa is called after the *stōa poikilē*, the 'coloured hall of columns' in the Athenian Agora where its founder, Zeno, taught. The Stoics of the imperial period, with Seneca and Epictetus as their main representatives, made ethics the definite centre of their thinking, and also succeeded in clothing their doctrinal structure in religious linguistic patterns, speaking often of providence and the divine will. This applies also to the pursuit of their main goal, viz. initiation into the correct manner of life and into coping with misadventures, which were to be borne with 'stoic' equanimity. Luke had no doubt a more positive picture of the Stoics, but this too is a question of customary stereotypes rather than of genuine knowledge, as we shall see more clearly when Stoic concerns are touched upon in the Areopagus discourse.

Paul's activity provokes a double reaction in the philosophers (v. 18). As with the reaction to the Pentecost event, here one reaction is completely dismissive, while the other is more open. In the negative response which excludes any further dialogue, Paul is contemptuously called a 'sower of words', i.e. one who assembles knowledge not his own and attempts to put on a good show with the undigested harvest of this intellectual theft; in short, a 'babbler'. The second, more positive, opinion correctly grasps Paul's activity as proclamation and evangelisation (*katangellein* and *euangelizesthai*) with 'Jesus and the resurrection (*Anastasis*)' as its theme; this means that the christological kerygma, used only sparingly in the Areopagus discourse, had been part of Paul's preaching in the Agora. We find an attractive explanation of the striking juxtaposition of 'Jesus and the resurrection' as early as the church father John Chrysostom: Luke lets it appear that the Athenians are the victims of a misunderstanding. They imagine that Jesus and Anastasis are a divine pair consisting of a male and a female deity, on the analogy of Osiris and Isis from Egypt or Adonis and Atargatis from Asia Minor. This curious misunderstanding of the resurrection already sets its sights on the real problem which will cause a rupture at the close of the Areopagus discourse: the proclamation of the resurrection provokes misunderstandings and meets resistance, and there is not always as much reason to laugh as we find here.

It seems obvious that we should assign each reaction to one particular group: one Epicurean reaction, one Stoic reaction. Luke sees no further hope for the Epicureans, who have definitively turned their back on Paul with the contemptuous title 'babbler', whereas the Stoics at least display curiosity, so that they listen to his Areopagus discourse; some passages in this speech have a Stoic colouring, but it contains nothing that would be distinctively Epicurean. However, the immortality of the human being or of the human soul was an object of contention for both schools (in different ways: the Epicureans dismissed it out of hand, while representatives of the Stoa took more nuanced positions), and a resurrection of the body was unthinkable for both. It follows that the double reaction in v. 32 could be attributed to both groups. Intermediary positions may also have existed.

d. The Areopagus

Paul is now brought to the Areopagus for a further discussion (not a trial). The Are-o-pagus in Athens is the hill (*pagos*) of Ares, the god of war, lying between the Acropolis and the Pnyx, the place where assemblies of the people were held. There is not very much room on the hill itself, but the ridge leading up to the Acropolis would have been able to accommodate a larger number of hearers. The 'Areopagus' was however also the name of a committee, originally so called because it met as a kind of court on this hill. Later it moved to a building on the Agora, but retained the name. It is not clear where its competence lay; some authors write that it once again acquired greater importance in the Roman period and exercised supervision of religious worship, the sanctuaries, education and other matters. As the ministry in charge of religion and schools, it would thus be responsible for dealing with a 'proclaimer of new deities'. This, however, remains very uncertain.

Does Luke understand the 'Areopagus' as a place or a committee? Both interpretations can find support in his text. *Epi ton Areion pagon* can be translated either 'on to the Areopagus' or 'before the Areopagus'; the same applies to Paul's position 'in the middle of the Areopagus' in v. 22. Dionysius 'the Areopagite' in v. 34 must be a member of the committee, but this will hardly be the case with Damaris and some other new converts. These come from the larger public who have heard Paul along with the Stoics and the members of the Areopagus, and it is improbable that this has taken place anywhere else than on the hill of Ares: this argues in favour of understanding the term as designating a location. Luke found the designation 'Areopagite' in his source. This may have suggested the introduction of the Areopagus, something handy for Luke since it was a specific characteristic of Athens: every city of any importance had an Agora and an Acropolis, but only Athens had an Areopagus.

Verses 19f. continue the second, open reaction in v. 18 by formulating in direct speech the expectations addressed to Paul: 'May we know what this new teaching is which you present? For you bring some strange things to our ears; we wish to know therefore what these things mean.' Luke's narrative commentary in v. 21 is a further stroke in his portrait of the ideal (or not so ideal) Athens: 'Now all the Athenians and the foreigners who lived there spent their time in nothing except telling or hearing something new.' The curiosity of the Athenians was proverbial. Thucydides has Cleon tell them in a speech: 'You are slaves of the newest sensation to turn up, so you have no difficulty in welcoming a novel idea . . . You are addicted to the pleasure of hearing novelties and behave as if you were sitting in the theatre to enjoy those skilled in speaking.'[13] This curiosity includes an open ear for the new things offered in the market of worldviews. People wanted to investigate these, even if the motive was a desire to pass the time, rather than genuine existential interest. This bodes ill for the Christian proclamation: it is scarcely to be expected that it will touch the heart of this superficial people.

e. Modest success

Before we turn to the Areopagus speech in the following section, let us note here what Luke tells us in vv. 32–34 about its success and failure. When the hearers are confronted with the theme of resurrection and understandably enough take this to mean the general resurrection of the dead, not so much the resurrection of Jesus Christ, some of them react with total dismissal: they begin to mock. Another group says: 'We will hear you again about this.' One can indeed interpret this as a rejection clothed in polite words, but it does not exclude *a priori* the possibility of continuing the discussion. The fact that a postponement to a later occasion was all that could be attained from most of the hearers shows us where the boundaries lie. It is not possible to present the faith in its totality as an organic continuation of what people have believed up to now: rather, at one specific point it presupposes also risk, a decision, a break with the past and a fresh departure into something unknown.

The lapidary observation in v. 33, 'So Paul went out from among them', indicates that this time it is Paul himself who breaks off the disputation. He is not chased away, nor do the others move off and leave him alone: he himself takes the initiative. This does not of itself mean that Luke sees him as having failed. A further (third) reaction comes unexpectedly in v. 34, bringing the outcome Paul had hoped for. Some of his hearers join Paul and come to faith; and we should note that they do this without needing any miracle. Two of them are singled out: 'Dionysius the Areopagite and a woman named Damaris.' This accords with Luke's tendency to present pairs of characters (cf. e.g. Simeon and Anna in Lk 2:25–38).

If we assume that this information is reliable, it remains unclear what happened with these new Athenian converts. Did they form a house community which was too small to attract further attention in our sources? Did they leave Athens? The testimony of Paul's letters and the Acts of the Apostles is that the early Christians moved around a lot.

Dionysius achieved a swift career in Christian tradition.[14] Damaris became his wife, and Eusebius promoted him to first bishop of Athens. Under his name, there came into being in the fifth century a body of

---

[13] Thucydides, *History of the Peloponnesian War* 3.38, 4f.
[14] Cf. H. C. Graef, *LThK*, second edn III, 402f.; A. M. Ritter, *RGG*, fourth edn II, 859f.

mystical writings with a theology that exercised a great influence on the middle ages. He won increased authority through association with the Parisian martyr of the same name. It was only at the beginning of the modern period that cautious doubts began to be raised about these identifications, and not until the close of the nineteenth century that Catholic critics joined in the expression of these reservations.

If we look back over what has been said, we can see that Luke has succeeded with a few powerful strokes in painting an idealised picture of the city of Athens. The great institutions of the city, the shadow of Socrates, the most important philosophical schools of Luke's own period, the Agora as the place where people met and talked with one another, the great number of religious monuments, the well-known curiosity of the inhabitants of the city—all this combines to form a panorama that seems drawn directly from life, but this faithfulness in the detail is due to the skill of the author, who was more familiar with literature about Athens than with the real city. He employs the same care in his portrait of the city that he has earlier employed for persons such as Simon Magus or Bar-Jesus. In other words, this time it is the city that is the protagonist which offers the resistance with which Paul must deal.

3. The unknown god: the address on the Areopagus (Acts 17:22–31)

a. Captatio benevolentiae (vv. 22–23)

In keeping with the recommendations of the rhetorical handbooks of antiquity, Paul begins his speech with a *captatio benevolentiae*, i.e. a 'clutching at goodwill'. This is intended to elicit a friendly attitude in his hearers and to increase their attentiveness to what he will now tell them. Accordingly, after he has taken up the typical speaker's position in the middle of a half-circle, he says in v. 22: 'I perceive that in every way you are very religious.' But this compliment is not without its difficulties. The underlying Greek word *deisi-daimonia* covers a broad spectrum of meanings from the pious fear of God to crass superstition,[15] so that one could also translate: 'Your superstition is especially striking.' It was, of course, impossible for him to say this to his public: but here we have a good example of the distinction (which we have followed implicitly throughout this book) between narrated communication and communication via narration. The narrated communication takes place in the world of direct speech between Paul and the Athenians: here, Paul appears to be flattering them, and this is how the Athenians understand him. At the same time, however, this narrative effects a communication between the author and his readers. With a wink (so to speak) Luke lets the reader

---

[15] On *deisidaimōn* and *deisidaimonia*, cf. the more detailed study by H.-J. Klauck, 'Religion without Fear. Plutarch on Superstition and Early Christian Literature', *Skrif en Kerk* 18 (1997), 111–26.

understand that the allegedly so intelligent Athenians have not even noticed how poisoned this praise was, and he establishes a collusion between himself and those for whom he is writing, in regard to the problematic aspect of Gentile religiosity.

This double level of meaning suffices to avoid an excessively harsh contrast between Paul's anger in v. 16 at a city full of idols and the tactical device he employs in v. 22. Besides, the compliment refers only to what follows in v. 23. In the course of his ramblings through the city, Paul has also seen an altar with the inscription 'To an unknown god' or 'To the unknown god', and this is a welcome starting point for his discourse. Here we need to know whether it was in fact possible for Paul to see such an inscription in Athens and, if so, what its original meaning was.[16]

As yet, archaeological and literary evidence has been found only of altars with the inscription in the plural: 'To the unknown gods'; it is probable that the singular form did not exist. To be sure, our knowledge of antiquity is very far from complete, and it is theoretically possible that unfortunate accidents in transmission have robbed us of inscriptions in the singular. But the astonishment displayed by a man like Jerome, who was extremely well versed in classical culture and languages, makes it possible for us to check what Luke says. Jerome believes that Paul was the first to create the singular form, and that his reasons for so doing are transparent:

> The inscription of the altar was not, however—as Paul asserted—'To an unknown god', but rather: 'To the gods of Asia, Europe and Africa, the unknown and foreign gods.'[17]

We wish to contradict Jerome only on one point: it was not Paul, but Luke who made the alteration, thereby following a tendency also found in the interaction of hellenistic Judaism with classical poetical and philosophical texts. The singular 'god' was substituted for the plural 'gods' in the original, and the proper name 'Zeus' was replaced by the more abstract term 'god'. This gave a touch of monotheistic colour to Gentile texts, making it easier to employ them for purposes of propaganda and apologetics.

One might object here that there is no great difference between the plural and the singular. But a surreptitious transposition in meaning does in fact occur. The dedication of an altar to unknown gods is generated by the aim of embracing as many divine names as possible, and by the fear of forgetting one god; this applied especially to heroes, some of whom

---

[16] On this, cf. P. W. van der Horst, 'The Altar of the "Unknown God" in Athens (Acts 17:23) and the Cult of "Unknown Gods" in the Hellenistic and Roman Periods', *ANRW* II/18.2 (1989), 1426–56.

[17] Jerome, *Commentary on the Letter to Titus*, 1, 12 (Patrologia Latina 26, 607).

were anonymous. If gods are continually overlooked, they react in anger by punishing the human beings who refuse them the sacrifice that is their due. In order to be on the safe side, this system provides a neutral place. Every unnamed deity could feel addressed by the dedication of the altar (on the lines of 'to whom it may concern'). When Jerome also speaks of 'foreign gods', he draws our attention to a political dimension: these are the divinities of friendly and allied states. It was not possible to remember or pronounce their names, but they were assumed into the public worship of one's own city in order to intensify the political links and clothe these in the aura of the numinous.

At the close of v. 23, Luke evaluates this phenomenon, of which he himself is to some extent the creator, as follows: 'What therefore you worship as unknown, this I proclaim to you.' Already the neuter term is striking: 'what you worship', not 'whom you worship'. Thus, Luke is careful not to import a clearly outlined personal concept of God into the altar inscription. He sees the presence of a premonition on the part of the human soul, but one cannot uncover the essential contents of the Christian proclamation merely by reflection on the religious traditions of humanity. This boundary is also indicated by the mention of ignorance, implicitly in v. 27 and explicitly in v. 30. This ignorance can be overcome only by the Christian proclamation, with its summons to repentance.

Finally, there is also a concealed biblical dimension present when Luke writes of the unknown god, since he is at the same time the hidden God of whom Old Testament prophecy speaks: 'Truly, you are a hidden God, O God of Israel, the saviour!' (Is 45:15). This inspires the prophet to hope that the Egyptians, Ethiopians and Sabaeans will come to Israel and confess: 'God is with you only, and there is no other' (Is 45:14). The hidden God emerges from his hiddenness when he acts; he is made known in preaching and wants to be acknowledged by all, for otherwise judgement threatens. In terms of the narrative framework, we also discover that there is a gap in the Gentiles' own structure of faith, a space left empty for the 'foreign divinities' whom Paul is allegedly preaching (cf. Acts 17:18). But it is the Bible that supplies the matter to fill this.

We shall frequently have occasion to repeat the observation that most of the affirmations in the Areopagus discourse can be attested both in hellenistic (especially Stoic) thinking and in the Old Testament. Luke takes diaspora Judaism as his model in his attempt to create a bridge between these two spheres, and his virtuosity partly succeeds in doing so. References to the theology of creation dominate the beginning of the speech; next, borrowings from philosophy come into the foreground; only in the final verse do we find a reserved formulation of the early Christian kerygma, which determines the selection and structuring of the material as a whole.

b. The Creator needs nothing (vv. 24–25)

The next little section, which is the beginning of the main part of the discourse, opens with affirmations about the creation: God made the world and everything in it (cf. Ex 20:11; Is 45:18), so that he is the Lord who rules over heaven and earth (cf. Tob 7:17). The conclusion of the verse states that he upholds everything, since he bestows on everything the vital force and the breath of life (cf. Is 42:5, 'Thus says God, the Lord, who created the heavens and stretched them out, who spread forth the earth and what comes from it, who gives *breath* to the people upon it and *spirit* to those who walk in it . . .'). By employing here at the beginning of v. 24 the term *kosmos* for the 'world', rather than the word *gē*, which is more common in the Old Testament, Luke establishes a point of contact with Stoic cosmology, which however tends to equate the world, as the totality of all that exists, with God (see below).

Creation theology supplies the basis for the formulation of two or three points of criticism: God does not dwell in temples built by human hands, nor does he let himself be served by human beings, since one must avoid giving the impression that God requires something for his existence. The first point immediately calls to mind the criticism of the temple in Stephen's preaching (cf. Acts 7:48–50), but we should also consider the relativising words in a passage from Solomon's prayer at the dedication of the temple: 'But will God indeed dwell on the earth? Behold, heaven and the highest heaven cannot contain you; how much less this house which I have built!' (1 Kgs 8:27). Psalm 50:12f. attacks the view that God is dependent for his survival on sacrifices: 'If I were hungry, I would not tell you; for the world and all that is in it is mine. Do I eat the flesh of bulls, or drink the blood of goats?' But the Epicurean and Stoic criticism of public worship also drew on this insight, generated by their experience of the forms in which piety was practised: statues of the gods were clothed in precious garments, they were anointed and decorated and laid on banqueting sofas, and then meals were set before them. The following passage in Seneca attacks this practice:[18]

> We should like to forbid the morning levée and sitting at the temple gates: human pride lets itself be ensnared by such exercises of religious duty. The god is honoured by one who knows him. We should like to forbid offering linen garments and a stiff brush to Jupiter, and holding up a mirror to Juno: the god needs no domestic servants. And why is this so? Because he himself serves the human race, he is present everywhere and to everyone . . . It is the gods who direct the course of the world, who order the universe with their power, and maintain the human race in existence.

[18] *Moral Letters*, 95, 47 and 50.

It is obvious that Judaism and Christianity could agree with this critique, though not with the associated picture of the world. Naturally, the intention was not to prohibit human persons from venerating God, but rather to reject naive, excessively anthropomorphic images that people had made of God; and this applies to all attempts to take possession of God (so to speak) and use him for one's own ends.

c. The vocation of humankind (vv. 26–27)

Luke begins v. 26 with the statement that God 'made from *one* every nation of men'. When the official German Catholic translation renders the Greek: 'From one single human being he created the entire human race,' it imports an interpretation into the text. Luke no doubt does have Adam in mind, as the ancestor of the human race (cf. Lk 3:28), but he intentionally leaves out the personal name here, for two reasons. First, foreign names which convey no meaning to Paul's hearers would make excessive demands of them; secondly, 'one' could be understood not only as a masculine term, but also as neuter, making possible a Stoic interpretation—everything has come into being from one primal principle.

The first goal laid down for human beings as a consequence of this is to 'live on all the face of the earth' (v. 26), recalling the charge given at creation (Gen 1:28). This in turn is explained by saying that God has 'determined allotted periods and the boundaries of their habitation'. Jer 5:22–24 helps us to interpret these words: the Lord 'placed the sand as the bound for the sea, a perpetual barrier which it cannot pass', and it is he who 'gives the rain in its season, the autumn rain and the spring rain, and keeps for us the weeks appointed for the harvest.' We may also compare Ps 74:17, 'You have fixed all the bounds of the earth; you have made summer and winter.' Thus the 'allotted times' refer to the seasons of the year, as in Acts 14:17. The 'boundaries of their habitation' is an echo of the account of creation: God has first to conquer the chaotic powers of the primal flood, before he can shape the earth and give human beings the fruitful land of fields and pastures. Other interpreters understand this text not in terms of the theology of creation, but in terms of political philosophy: the 'times' would refer to historical periods, and the spaces indicated would refer to states with stable boundaries. If this idea is present at all, however, it is only a secondary component, in the sense that a philosophically-trained public could read the text in this way and so be led to the primary affirmation Luke makes about God's working in creation.

The second goal laid down is formulated very cautiously in v. 27 as the instruction given to human beings to 'seek God, in the hope that they might feel after him and find him' (two optatives in Greek). In the Greek Bible, the rare verb 'feeling after' refers *inter alia* to the fumbling and groping of blind persons in the dark. The search for God is also one of the great themes of the Old Testament: 'You will seek the Lord your God, and you will find him, if you search after him with all your heart and with all your soul' (Deut 4:29; this is preceded by Israel's backsliding into idol-worship); 'Seek the Lord while he may be found, call upon him while he is near' (Is 55:6). But before this search can take place, God must first reveal himself. Through his action in Israel's history, he has disclosed himself to those to whom he speaks in these texts, demanding that they respond through existential conversion to him. But things are different with those to whom Paul speaks in his Areopagus discourse: here, nothing more seems possible than the notion of a distant God, and the yearning for him which Luke sees documented in the altar inscription.

Luke is in accord here with the Book of Wisdom, which provides a common background of tradition for both himself and Paul. The premise of the unknown author is that 'from the greatness and beauty of created things comes a corresponding perception of their Creator' (Wis 13:5). The author seems at first almost to excuse the Greek thinkers who have not wholly succeeded in achieving this perception: 'Yet these men are little to be blamed, for perhaps they go astray while seeking God and desiring to find him' (13:6). But then he fires the accusing question at them: 'If they had the power to know so much that they could investigate the world, how did they fail to find sooner the Lord of these things?' (13:9). The Book of Wisdom notes the existence of a kind of fundamental religiosity in the human person, a *desiderium naturale* in scholastic terminology, which can ascend via the critique of worship and of religion to catch sight of an unknown God—but also tends continually to take false paths. It suffices to read only one Stoic reflection on these problems, part of the *Olympian Discourse* of Dio Chrysostom. There are a number of striking points of contact with ideas which we have encountered in the Areopagus discourse, but here the 'groping' refers directly to statues of the gods:

> No one would wish to maintain that it would be better not to provide human beings with any image or picture of the gods, on the grounds that they ought to look only at the phenomena which appear in the heavens. A rational human being venerates all of these and takes them to be blessed gods, even though he only sees them from afar. But all human beings are oriented towards the divine, so that they are driven by a powerful yearning to venerate the god from close at hand, serving him, drawing close to him, touching him with full conviction, sacrificing to him and decking him with garlands. For human beings behave towards the gods in exactly the same way as little children who are separated from their father and mother: these experience an irresistible longing for their parents and stretch out their hands yearningly to them in dreams, although the parents are not in fact present. Human beings are right to love the gods for the benefits they have received and because they are

related to them, and they wish in every way to be with the gods and enjoy their company. This is why many foreign peoples, who are poor and lack artistic skill, attribute the name of gods to mountains, unpruned trees and shapeless stones, although such things bear no more resemblance to the gods than does the human form (*Or.* 12.60f.).

Verse 27 gives one final reason for human seeking and finding, viz. the affirmation that God 'is not far from each one of us'. We have already seen in Is 55:6, quoted above, that God is near to us, and Ps 145:18 likewise says: 'The Lord is near to all who call upon him.' But this idea introduces the transition to the Stoic quotation in v. 28, and it is not by chance that we find a close parallel in Seneca, who in his *Moral Epistles* tells his correspondent Lucilius:

One need not lift one's hands to heaven nor implore the temple guardian to give us access to the ear of the divine statue, as though our prayer would be better heard there: *the god is near you, he is with you, he is in you.* This is my conviction, Lucilius: a sacred spirit dwells in us, observing and watching over our evil and good deeds: as we treat him, so he treats us. But without the god, no one is a good human being; or is there anyone with the power to raise himself above destiny, unless he is supported by the god? There are decisions which are generous and honest: in every good person there dwells a god, though it is uncertain which god this is (*Ep.* 41, 1f.).

d. Humankind as related to the divine (vv. 28–29)

We have just heard Seneca say that the god is near us, indeed that he is in us. Verse 28 shows the reverse order: 'For in him we live and move and have our being.' This triad of life, movement and existence may perhaps refer to the various degrees of being classified by the natural philosophy of antiquity: plants too possess life, while animals can also move, but only the human being has intellectual existence as well. There is not in fact a literal verbal parallel to this passage, but its components are found in early Greek philosophy, in the reflections about the being and the significance of Zeus, the highest god. We find them in the fifth line of the Stoic hymn to Zeus (see below), but also at an earlier date in Plato's dialogue about the coming into existence of the world, the *Timaeus* (10 [37c]): 'When now the father who had begotten the universe saw this image of the eternal gods filled with movement and life, he rejoiced, and this joy led him to make it resemble the archetype even more.' Luke, however, has already introduced a similar triad at the close of v. 25, when he defines 'life and breath and everything' as the gift of the biblical God of creation. This means that he does not seriously intend his formula in v. 28 to be understood as a mythological or philosophical (Platonic or Stoic) affirmation. If we are to translate the text as Luke means it to be understood, we should not write: 'in him', but rather: 'through him' (which is perfectly possible in terms of grammar). We live through God, i.e. we have received our existence from the hand of the Creator, and it is he who sustains our life.

The following Stoic fragment is introduced by a specific quotation formula: 'As even some of your poets have said'. We should not make too much of the fact that this plural—'some poets'—is used to introduce only one line of a poem, since this may be nothing more than a conventional stylistic device; it is however worth noting that the contents of the quotation can be adduced in at least two texts. By saying 'your poets', Paul, who stands on biblical-Jewish ground, distances himself from those who are listening to his speech, as well as from obvious but undesirable implications of the quotation. Nevertheless, the quotation-formula is parallel to the introduction of quotations from the Old Testament, e.g. at Acts 13:33, 'As also it is written in the second psalm', or 7:48, 'As the prophet says'. The apostle attempts to refute his Jewish hearers on the basis of the Bible, which speaks about Christ, and to win them over; before a Gentile crowd, the task of persuasion invokes the aid of affirmations by their own poets and thinkers, who open up an initial path of access to the true concept of God.

The Greek text of the quotation is metrical, a half hexameter with three accents, *tóu gar kaí genos ésmen*, which we might reproduce in English as: 'Fór we are hís familý.' It comes from the *Phenomena* ('Heavenly Epiphanies'), a didactic poem by Aratus of Soloi (third century BCE), from which we quote the first lines:

> Let us begin with God! Human beings should never cease
> to pronounce his name, since the city streets are full of God,
> as are all human markets, likewise the sea
> and its harbours. We need the help of God everywhere—
> *for we are indeed his offspring!* Lovingly, he sends human beings
> signs that mean good; he wakens the peoples so they can work,
> exhorting them to find food; he teaches when the field is ready
> to be ploughed by oxen and hoed, and when the time
> is propitious for planting and sowing all kinds of seeds.

This text is transmitted to us from two directions. The Jewish author Aristobulus used it to introduce his Gentile readers to biblical mono-theism, and Eusebius has preserved fragments of his work in the *Praeparatio Evangelica*, which seeks to elaborate programmatic points of contact for the proclamation of the gospel in the Gentile world of antiquity. There is scarcely any distinction in Greek between this text and the first half of the fourth line of the celebrated hymn to

Zeus composed by Cleanthes, one of the founding fathers of the Stoic school:[19]

> Highest, omnipotent God, named by many names,
> Zeus, lord of nature, who govern the universe according to law,
> all hail! It is fitting for mortal human beings to praise you.
> *For we are indeed all your offspring*, and we alone,
> of all that lives and moves here on earth, are endowed with speech.
> Therefore will I praise you, and ever proclaim your power.

It is not difficult to explain how Luke got hold of Stoic ideas. He may have known them from his education at school, he may have taken them from anthologies of Stoic commonplaces such as these, or he may have adopted them from Jewish apologetics (cf. Aristobulus). It is more important to be clear about how the Stoics on the one hand, and Luke on the other, understood the contents of these words. In the Stoa, this quotation and the preceding triad have their place in a general materialistic and pantheistic framework. In other words, the Stoa thinks in unitary terms of the totality of Being, deriving all that exists from one single abstract world-principle; they postulated a kind of subtle fire as the materialistic substratum of this world-principle. This means that the Stoics can explain the world in unitary terms: nothing exists outside this world and its material basis—no external power, no world of ideas, no transcendent god. As far as the concept of god is concerned, this necessarily leads to pantheism: the things called 'gods' are components of this world, inner-worldly forces, distinct from humankind not in principle but only in degree, in the sense that distinctions exist among individual existents with regard to the realisation, the concentration or the purity of the primal matter which governs all things. A religious cipher such as 'Zeus' can be used to designate the governing principle, but this may equally be called the world-reason (*logos*), providence (*pronoia*), or world-spirit (*pneuma*). Where no distance separates one from a transcendent creator god, it is correspondingly easier to speak (as our quotation does) of an essential relatedness between gods and humans.

In the early imperial period, the significance of the Stoa lay above all in the field of ethics. To some extent, this was detached from the philosophical presuppositions and integrated into a general humane ethos which in its essentials was also adopted by Christianity. Apart from this, we should mention that Stoicism also possessed an eschatology: periodically, at intervals of several thousand years, the world perishes in a great conflagration (the *ekpyrōsis*, world-fire). Only Zeus, the highest

---

[19] On both texts, cf. B. Effe, *Hellenismus* (Die griechische Literatur in Text und Darstellung 4) (Reclams Universal-Bibliothek 8064), Stuttgart 1985, 136f., 156f.; on Cleanthes' hymn, cf. A. A. Long and D. N. Sedley, *The Hellenistic Philosophers*, Cambridge 1987, I, 326f.; II, 326f.

god, survives this stream of fire to set up a new beginning. Our first reaction here is surprise: does there then exist a god outside the world? No, for ultimately, Zeus is identical with the fire; we could also say that Zeus is only another name for the fire which provides the matter out of which the new world comes into being.

Has Luke been seduced here by a strategic advantage into betraying the Christian concept of God and man, which insists on the distinction between the two? Certainly not. Basically, all he adopts is the verbal garment, not the underlying contents, nor the intellectual presuppositions. The quotation suggests to Luke a biblical model, viz. the human person's similarity to God in the first creation narrative. However, he deliberately refrains from speaking directly of this, just as he refrains from mentioning the name of Adam. He wishes to preserve the possibility of a consensus, even if only a rather external consensus. This brings him respectably close to Philo of Alexandria and the later church fathers.

Verse 29 draws a conclusion from the triad and the quotation: we ought not to think that the divine is like statues of gold, or silver, or stone, the products of human skill and ingenuity which are presented as images of the gods. Paul's anger at seeing the city full of idols, mentioned in the narrative framework (v. 16), and his critique of temples within the discourse itself (vv. 24f.), are now continued by an explicit critique of images. Once again, Luke could be sure that the philosophical schools would agree with his criticism of common religious practice, which is intensified by the Old Testament prohibition of images. Comparable polemic against idols is found at Is 40:18–20 and 44:9–20, but once again the Book of Wisdom is especially relevant. Immediately after the verses quoted above (Wis 13:5–9), the author continues his argument: 'But miserable, with their hopes set on dead things, are the men who give the name "gods" to the works of men's hands, gold and silver fashioned with skill, and likenesses of animals, or a useless stone, the work of an ancient hand' (13:10).

The logic of Luke's argument remains somewhat unclear, since from the fact that the human person is related or similar to God it is possible to infer that an anthropomorphic portrayal of the divine would be particularly appropriate. Here too, Wis 15:16f. sheds more light on our subject:

> For a man made them [the images of the gods], and one whose spirit is borrowed formed them; for no man can form a god which is like himself. He is mortal, and what he makes with lawless hands is dead, for he is better than the objects which he worships, since he has life, but they never have.

The comparison and contrast are based on the aliveness and vitality which God breathed into humankind (Gen 2:7). This act cannot be imitated by human persons. Since it lies outside their possibilities, all they can fashion are lifeless images, inferior to humankind themselves. Consequently, it would be no realisation of their relatedness to God, but rather a perversion, if they were to worship these as a representation of the divine.

e. Eschatological perspective (vv. 30–31)

The two concluding verses complete the three temporal phases of past, present and (eschatological) future. Paul calls the past in v. 30 'the times of ignorance' which God 'overlooked'; we may compare 14:16, 'In past generations he allowed all the nations to walk in their own ways.' Until now, God has been lenient, but this does not amount to a complete declaration of innocence, since human beings have also been guilty of error and confusion, by not making the best use of what was available to them. As in the Book of Wisdom, various degrees of ignorance are distinguished. Wis 13:6 speaks first of the natural philosophers who deserve only a light rebuke, then we hear in 13:10 of those whose situation is less happy, since they place their hope in images of the gods; finally, at 15:18, the worship of 'the most hateful animals' is mentioned as the most perverse behaviour of all. Luke sees ignorance as covering all the forms of religious practice which have been mentioned in the discourse: the city full of idols (v. 16) and the fashioning of statues of the gods from precious metals and stone (v. 29) which are then set up in temples and served with food (vv. 24f.). But a verbal link means that 'ignorance' (*agnoia*) also covers the altar inscription to an unknown (*agnōstos*) god. If we employ the categories of the Book of Wisdom, we can say that one who goes only as far as this deserves a lighter rebuke, since a point of contact is established for a dim perception of the creator God. But the situation is different for one who has encountered the true God in the lived faith of the Jewish people and in the Christian proclamation, but fails to know him and acknowledge him: such conduct is especially inexcusable (cf. Wis 13:8).

The present time is defined by the proclamation, in which more is involved than a simple switch from ignorance to the knowledge of God. Rather, God 'commands' (*parangellein*, related to *katangellein* and *euangelizesthai*, 'to proclaim') everyone to reform their thoughts, i.e. to give their thinking a new orientation, and to undergo conversion, i.e. to abandon false paths and set out on the correct path. The term *metanoia*, 'conversion', includes both of these, depending on whether one sees it more against its Greek background (as seems appropriate in a speech addressed to a Gentile public) or connects it rather to the demand for conversion made in Judaism, in the preaching of John the Baptist, and by Jesus. A reflection on one's life and a new definition of one's entire project for living are required. The best opportunity for this is provided by the present time, in which one can hear the message of the gospel. It is impossible not to hear the note of warning here: God's leniency is in fact over, and one must stop putting it to the test.

This warning is intensified by the concluding verse, which looks ahead to the final judgement: God 'has fixed a day on which he will judge the world in righteousness by a man whom he has appointed, and of this he has given assurance to all men by raising him from the dead' (v. 31). A link is established here between the Day of the Lord, invoked by the prophets in their proclamation of judgement, and the annunciation of God's universal act of judgement, e.g. in Ps 9:8, 'He judges the world with righteousness, he judges the peoples with equity.' The man 'appointed' is none other than Jesus Christ, who will come again (Acts 1:11) as the judge in the end-time. We already know why his name is not mentioned explicitly: the Areopagus discourse consistently refrains from employing Jewish-Christian proper names and designations which would as yet be too foreign to the (fictitious) public. When he states that God has authenticated (*pistin paraskhōn*) this Jesus, Luke uses a phrase from everyday speech which, however, includes the noun *pistis*, 'faith' or 'certification'. Thus he introduces, incidentally, a concept which the reader is intended to fill out with theological and christological substance, on the basis of the context in Acts 17.

This authentication takes place by means of the resurrection of Jesus Christ from the dead. Not only is this a final chord which lets the discourse as a whole flow into the central theme of Christian preaching; Luke also provides a harmonious agreement between the discourse itself and the narrative framework. The preaching of the resurrection has already provoked a strange misunderstanding on the part of those who heard it (v. 18). In v. 32, those addressed by the Areopagus discourse once again pick up this word, but now they understand it somewhat differently, relating it no longer to the raising of Jesus, but to the raising of the dead. The Christian conviction, which Luke also brings into the picture, links the two: the resurrection of Jesus is announced against the background of the apocalyptic expectation of the general resurrection of the dead, and the raising of one individual, namely Jesus, sets in motion the processes which lead to the raising of all the dead (cf. 1 Cor 15).

f. Controversies in the evaluation of this text

In his great academic dissertation *Paulus auf dem Areopag* ('Paul on the Areopagus', 1939), Martin Dibelius expressed a very negative theological judgement of the Areopagus discourse:[20] as 'a *hellenistic* address on the topic of the true *knowledge of God*', it is an 'alien' or 'foreign' body' in the New Testament as regards 'the manner of its expression and the development of its thought'. It is silent about 'the claim which

[20] Cf. M. Dibelius, *Aufsätze*, 29–70; quotations from 54f., 59, 65, 70.

the Christian message makes: that it is only thanks to revelation that it possesses the true knowledge of God, and can communicate this'. In this discourse, repentance 'ultimately consists in reflection on that knowledge of God which the human person possesses by nature', and Luke understands the word of the apostle 'not so much as the pronouncing of judgement over the lost situation of the Gentiles, but rather as the fulfilment of a yearning of which they themselves had hitherto been unconscious'. In short, 'the main ideas of the speech, about human knowledge of God and relatedness to God, are Stoic, not Christian'.

Subsequent research has made sizeable corrections to this assessment. Luke may perhaps not have reflected on all the implications, when he accepted the premises of popular hellenistic philosophy as far as his use of language is concerned; he was insufficiently aware that some of his prominent affirmations are anchored in the materialistic and pantheistic system elaborated by Stoic thought. But he has clearly ruled out an unchecked development in this direction: the philosophy of religion does not supply sufficient help to enable one to arrive at the genuine substance of the Christian proclamation. The unknown God remains unknown, unless the kerygma provides the answer to a question which otherwise would not be heard. It is not enough to reflect: a profound change in thinking, a repentance, is required, viz. insight into one's involvement in sin and a new existential orientation.

Luke intends the statements with a Stoic colouring to be read against the background of the first part of the discourse, which lays foundations drawn from the theology of creation. Then the reader will hear the intended echoes of the human similarity to God in the first creation narrative and the prohibition of images in the Old Testament. Diaspora Judaism, and especially the Book of Wisdom, had prepared the ground here, and Luke (like Paul himself) builds gratefully on these foundations.

The difference in substance between Luke and Paul is not so great as is often claimed. We have already drawn a comparison between 1 Thess 1:9 and the missionary sermon in Lystra: the demand made in 1 Thessalonians to abandon idols and turn to the true and living God confirms the kinds of affirmation represented in the Areopagus discourse (in a more reserved manner) by the critique of temples, public worship and images. According to 1 Thess 1:10, however, Paul's initial preaching had also a second part: the newly converted were to wait for Jesus, the Son of God, whom God had raised from the dead and who would come from heaven to save believers from the wrath to come. This second step was missing in the sermon at Lystra, but the Areopagus discourse supplies the gap by means of the eschatological prospect of its final verse. The similarities between Paul and Luke are due to their mutually independent recourse to material drawn from the diaspora synagogues and from the tradition of the early Christian communities.

Scholars who seek to establish an incompatibility between the Lukan and the Pauline conceptions appeal above all to Rom 1:18–32, where Paul proclaims God's wrath to the Gentiles and seems to have nothing good at all to say about paganism. But Paul's thesis that the Gentiles are inexcusable (Rom 1:20) is also found in Wis 13:8, in the middle of a passage that inspired Luke when he elaborated the motif of ignorance; and Rom 1:18–32 is followed immediately by an equally harsh attack on Judaism (Rom 2:1–3:20). This attack is the real goal of Paul's affirmations in 1:18–32. Some of the differences in tone can be explained by the different intentions of the authors: while Paul is preaching in a prophetical tone about judgement, Luke is offering an example of how to lay the preliminary basis for proclaiming the Christian God to Gentiles. To employ a metaphor, both are playing in the same key, but whereas Paul chooses dissonances and *fortissimo*, Luke prefers smooth triadic chords and *piano*.

In theological categories, what Luke is doing here expresses the tension between inculturation and evangelisation. The adaptation of Stoic thought in order to describe anew the biblical faith in the Creator is an example of the inculturation of the gospel, its translation into the modes of expression proper to a new and foreign world. However, this does not cause Luke to lose sight of the other pole, viz. the evangelisation of cultures, which involves subjecting the forms of Gentile religion to a critique generated by the gospel.

We have as yet paid insufficient attention to the function of the Areopagus discourse as a literary product within the entire project of Acts. Just as Luke puts a model discourse in the synagogue on Paul's lips at 13:16–40 and a model sermon to a Christian community at 20:18–35, so here he entrusts Paul with what he sees as a model of missionary proclamation to Gentiles. But these identifications of the various audiences refer only to the interactions of the characters in the narrated world of the text. They cannot be transposed to the context within which Acts was read and used. Acts addresses a Christian public, and consequently the same is true of the Areopagus discourse. Luke does not in the least intend the event in the past, which is awakened to life by being narrated, to function in his own days as a model for preaching to Greek philosophers. Rather, it is intended to strengthen the self-assurance of his Christian readers: 'The discourse on the Areopagus is a *Christian reflection* on the "natural" implications of *Christian discourse* in the context of the hellenistic educational tradition', and its aim 'is to embolden the reader in his understanding of the faith as against his own anxious suspicion that he may be philosophically backward.'[21] Within the narrative, Paul does not succeed in establishing communication with the philosophers of Athens, but this will be realised within the Christian

---

[21] K. Löning, 'Gottesbild', 106f.

community. Believers recognise that their faith can find a point of contact
with a naturally existing religious dimension of human existence, though
the faith is not simply identical with this dimension. Luke indicates to
such readers that belief in God is no offence against reason and every
philosophical insight. This stabilises their identity in the face of potential
mockery from without, and even more so against the quiet inward un-
easiness they themselves might feel on this topic.

VI

PAUL IN EPHESUS (ACTS 19)

After leaving Athens, Paul arrives in Corinth (Acts 18:1), where he meets with greater success and remains for about a year and a half (18:11) before travelling on to Ephesus (18:19). Ephesus, the capital of the senatorial province of Asia Minor and the seat of a proconsul, was one of the largest, most important and richest cities of the Mediterranean world in the first century of the Common Era.[1] The second great missionary journey of the apostle Paul, after several extensive detours (18:22f.), ends in Ephesus, where he remains for two years (19:10). His farewell journey, which will take him via Macedonia, Greece, Asia Minor and the islands to Caesarea and imprisonment at Jerusalem, begins at Acts 19:21f. with a programmatic introduction which matches the beginning of the narrative of Jesus' journey to Jerusalem (Lk 9:51f.); the definitive departure (Acts 20:1) is delayed by the uprising of the silversmiths (19:23–40).

During the two years, Paul speaks first in the synagogue (19:8) and then in the lecture-room of a man called Tyrannus, an activity that makes him look somewhat like a philosopher. The proclamation of the word comes first; only at 19:11f. does his miraculous activity take centre-stage.

1. *Miracle and magic: a difficult demarcation (Acts 19:11–20)*

At 19:11–20, Luke once again employs his well-tried alternation between standard setting and special effect. Summary information about Paul's miracles in 19:11f. and about magical practices and books of magic in 19:18f. frame the dramatic episode of an unsuccessful exorcism (19:13–16). The reaction to the 'exorcism' in v. 17 effects a transition to the theme of magic, and a note about growth rounds the text off. What Luke had to work on, apart from dry indications of place and time and his general religious or cultural knowledge, was surely the farcical nucleus related in vv. 13–16; it is not even certain whether this material was originally Christian.

---

[1] On the city, cf. H. Koester (ed.), *Ephesos: Metropolis of Asia. An Interdisciplinary Approach to Archaeology, Religion, and Culture* (HThS 41), Valley Forge, Pa. 1995; on the text, cf. R. Strelan, *Paul, Artemis, and the Jews in Ephesus* (BZNW 80), New York 1996; M. Fieger, *Im Schatten der Artemis: Glaube und Ungehorsam in Ephesus*, Berne et al. 1998.

a. The apostle's laundry (vv. 11–12)[2]

'God did extraordinary miracles by the hands of Paul' (v. 11). This introduction intends not only to present Paul as a superior worker of miracles, but also to ward off potential misunderstandings. Paul is not to give the impression of being some religious superman whose works display a perfect power and might of his own. Rather, God guides the hand that Paul lays on the sick to heal them. Those who see this have a practical idea (v. 12): instead of all the effort required to transport their sick to Paul, they find a way to conserve Paul's miraculous power and take it home to the sufferers, using *sudaria*, i.e. sweat-cloths that Paul wore on his head, and *simicinctia*, loin-cloths or aprons or even handkerchiefs that had come into contact with Paul's skin. When these are laid upon the patients, success ensues: illnesses disappear and evil spirits come forth.

Theodor Zahn has made a charming attempt to defuse the basic question which this narrative imperiously prompts: 'The relatives of the sick will have succeeded in persuading Priscilla, in whose house Paul was staying, to lend them some head-cloth or handkerchief or other, which they would have returned immediately.'[3] But this cannot divert us from the fundamental problem: it appears that the miraculous power is thought of in material terms, so that it can be 'tapped' from the person of the wonder-worker and stored for subsequent use. The cloths take on the function of the amulets and talismans which were so common in the magic of antiquity. Nor is it sufficient to be told that Luke intends here to give Paul a position equal to that of Peter, whose shadow works miracles when it falls on the sick (Acts 5:15), and that both of them are followers of Jesus here: the crowd pressed upon him to touch him, in order to get some portion of his miraculous power (Lk 6:19), and the woman with a flow of blood succeeded in this, when she touched the hem of his garment (Lk 8:44).

We must begin by agreeing with Luke that all these phenomena are externally very similar, and therefore remain ambiguous. There exist only a few criteria for discernment; one of these is always the refusal to accept payment, but this idea is not put directly into words in Acts 19. Ultimately, it is all a question of interpretation: what are the relational coordinates of the specific action, and what system of convictions is involved? The understanding of miracles in v. 12 is located in dangerous border territory, and Luke intends to direct it into correct theological channels by means of his reference to God's working (v. 11), which presents the human messenger as only an instrument. The same aim is served by the earlier mention of the 'kingdom of God'

---

[2] Cf. S. Schreiber, *Paulus als Wundertäter*, 99–108.
[3] T. Zahn, *Apg*, 681f.

(v. 8): just as with Jesus, so Paul's miracles make the salvation promised by this kingdom a concrete reality. Bearing in mind the often very abstract and colourless way in which salvation is proclaimed, it is surely good that here the bodily, earthly dimension of salvation also receives its due.

b. The unsuccessful exorcism (vv. 13–16)

A number of motifs from exorcism narratives are included in the unsuccessful attempt at exorcism (vv. 13–16): the demon's attempted resistance, its superhuman knowledge, the immense physical strength of the possessed man, the significance attached to the name. The first point which we shall consider is the information in v. 13 that Jesus and Paul were not the only ones with power to expel demons: there were also other professionals who issued orders to spirits, especially Jewish exorcists, whose existence is hinted at in the Gospel (Lk 9:49 and 11:19). Flavius Josephus too is familiar with them; he describes how a Jew named Eleazar employed recipes by Solomon to treat a possessed man before the emperor Vespasian, making a tremendous impression upon those present.[4] The special characteristic in this case is that these exorcists employ the name of Jesus as a means to command the spirits—something that reminds us of the Jewish magician Bar-Jesus. We learn this twice, both in the narrative itself and in the direct quotation of the formula employed: 'I adjure you by the Jesus whom Paul preaches.'

Why is the name of Jesus adopted as a mere instrument of magic? Jesus and his disciples had the reputation of successful miracle-workers, and others desired to unlock their secrets and profit from them. Magicians sometimes claimed to conjure up the spirits of persons who had recently died and to use the power of the dead for their own purposes; this could lead to the suspicion that the disciples of Jesus achieved their effects by uttering the name of Jesus—who was dead—in order to conjure up his spirit. At any rate, it seemed a good idea to imitate what they were doing. Historically speaking, there is in principle nothing inconceivable about non-Christians (to say nothing of Christians themselves) abusing the name of Jesus for magical aims. In later magical papyri, we find texts such as the following:

A good remedy for those possessed by demons . . . Take oil from unripe olives with the plants *mastigia* and *lotometra*, and cook it with colourless marjoram . . . Write the protective device on a little tablet of tin and hang it around the neck of the sufferer: every demon will be terrified by this, since he fears it. The spell runs as follows: 'By the God of the Hebrews, I adjure you, Jesus, you who appear in fire, you who are in the midst of field and

---

[4] Flavius Josephus, *Antiquitates Judaicae* ('Jewish Antiquities') 8, 42–9.

snow and mist; may your inexorable angel descend and bind fast the wandering demon of this creature . . .[5]

Verse 14 makes the transition from the general description of the situation in v. 13 to the specific case in Ephesus: 'Seven sons of a Jewish high priest named Sceva were doing this.' No high priest bearing this name, which is derived from the Latin Scaeva or Scaevola, ever existed, but it is not necessary to have recourse to half-hearted solutions which make these men the seven sons of a member of the priestly aristocracy in Jerusalem, or of a provincial priest of the imperial cult who had Jewish ancestry: this is a 'stage name' of the seven. In Judaism, only the high priest was allowed to utter the divine name under special circumstances, and it was supposed that priests were acquainted with hidden traditional knowledge. Juvenal caricatures a Jewish beggar-woman who traffics in interpretations of dreams as 'a handmaid of the laws of Jerusalem, high priestess of the tree and reliable messenger of the highest heaven'.[6] Thus, the Jewish exorcists present themselves as both venerable and competent heirs to the sacred skills of Judaism. The fact that there are seven of them—the holy number *par excellence*—serves only to underline their lack of success, especially in comparison with Paul, who performs exorcisms on his own. In other texts, we often find seven demons, rather than seven exorcists (Lk 8:2; 11:26); the reversal of the customary situation, seven against one rather than one against seven, does not help these seven exorcists at all.

In v. 15, the evil spirit even shows signs of a sense of humour. He is completely unmoved by the efforts of the self-appointed exorcists, and replies: 'Jesus I know, and Paul I know; but who are you?' This does not mean that he is unacquainted with the seven sons of Sceva; rather, he is dismissing every claim they make to authority as exorcists. Unlike Paul, they have usurped the name of Jesus, to which they have no rights, so that it is impossible for them to expel the demon, who stays put. More than this, the demon becomes aggressive: he bestows superhuman powers on the possessed man, who falls in a berserk fury upon the hapless exorcists, overpowers them and rains blows on them, so that they run away naked and wounded.

At the conclusion of our text, it seems as if the demon remains unperturbed and emerges as the winner. But this is true only *vis-à-vis* the sons of Sceva; according to the demon's own words, he would submit to Jesus and Paul. This trial of strength does not take place, however, since an initial goal has been attained. Anyone who wishes to misuse sacred Christian names for magical aims is labouring under a fundamental misunderstanding. The intended miracle will rebound on him and punish the plagiarist. This incident generates the reactions in the following verses.

[5] Papyri Graecae Magicae IV, 3007–27.
[6] Juvenal, *Satires*, 6, 542–7.

c. An end to magic! (vv. 17–20)

According to v. 17, news of this misfortune spreads among all the Jews and Greeks in Ephesus, just as v. 10 has earlier told us that the word of the Lord spread among the Jews and Greeks in Asia Minor. They react in awe to the presence of the numinous and praise with due respect the name of the Lord Jesus, which before had been abused. Verse 18 tells us: 'Many also of those who were now believers came, confessing and divulging their practices.' Who are these persons who have come to belief, and what kind of practices were these? The perfect participle in the Greek text indicates that 'those who had come to belief' have been members of the Christian community for some time already; they are not Jews and Greeks who enter the community only now, under the impact of these recent events. As for 'their practices', one should note that *praxis* is a standard term for magical acts. Thus, the unsuccessful exorcism has given even Christians food for thought and motivated them to admit that they themselves have practised magic or trusted to magical help. Naturally, they wish to do so no longer; the only question is, when this magical activity occurred. One possibility would be to situate it in the period before they came to faith: this would mean that these believers suddenly realise that they had not been fully open when they became Christians, and now want to put things right. The alternative is that these Christians, like Simon Magus, have lapsed into magical practices, and now wish to put an end to these by means of an unreserved confession. This second possibility must at least remain open; indeed, it almost seems as if Luke consciously refrains from expressing himself more precisely.

This lack of precision continues in the transition to v. 19: 'And a number of those who practised magic arts brought their books together and burned them in the sight of all; and they counted the value of them and found it came to fifty thousand pieces of silver.' It is difficult to decide whether the beginning of this verse refers to a completely new group, or whether these persons overlap at least in part with 'those who were now believers'. At any rate, there is a direct connection between the 'practices' and the magic practices (literally, the text means 'impertinent or inquisitive behaviour') and books. These books are parchment booklets and papyrus rolls with magical spells and formulae, directions for making amulets, etc. The so-called *Ephesia grammata* enjoyed proverbial status in the classical period. Plutarch observed: 'The magicians charge those possessed by demons to recite the Ephesian writings by themselves and to pronounce the names.'[7] Even though these papyrus strips with magical words were produced in Egypt, they have a verbal link to Ephesus; this is why Luke could use them to create local atmosphere. The emperor Augustus ordered two thousand magical books

---

[7] Plutarch, *Quaestiones Convivialium* ('Discussions at Table') 7.5, 4 (760e).

to be burnt;[8] but such burnings of books in antiquity always took place under compulsion, not voluntarily as here in Acts. Despite the high price fetched by good magical texts, the figure named by Luke is doubtless exaggerated. More important, however, is the link to a major Lukan theme: in this instance, the only appropriate expression of readiness to renounce one's possessions and follow Jesus is the destruction of these corrupting wares—not an action such as selling the books and giving the proceeds to the poor.

Thus the three textual elements in Acts 19:11–20 accord with the anti-magical line. The example in the middle of this passage is meant to show that it is not a good idea to attempt to compete with Christianity by adopting exclusively Christian concepts. Ultimately, this means that one must bid magic farewell altogether, and keep the new Christian life pure in the face of all risks posed by magic. This, however, does not lead to a vacuum, since the gap is filled by the Christian offer of meaning, which consists of the proclamation and of the miracles which accompany it and include the bodily dimension.

2. The revolt of the silversmiths (Acts 19:23–40)

Three individual scenes stand out in the long textual unit 19:23–40. A heading (v. 23) is followed in vv. 24–28 by the 'incendiary' speech of the silversmith Demetrius, which is framed by narrative notes and closes with the acclamation by the crowd: 'Great is Artemis of the Ephesians!' In the centre (vv. 29–34), we have a pure narrative, describing the tumult itself; this too ends with the acclamation: 'Great is Artemis of the Ephesians!' The final section (vv. 35–40) is occupied almost entirely by the great discourse of the town clerk, who succeeds in calming the crowd.

A number of awkward points in the middle section indicate that Luke, who himself is largely responsible for the speeches in Acts, has made use of a local Ephesian tradition in the structure of his narrative. For example, Paul is mentioned only in an aside during this commotion (vv. 30f.), and one may ask where he is all this time. Why are Gaius and Aristarchus especially affected (v. 29), and what is the significance of 'Alexander, whom the Jews had put forward' (vv. 32f.)? It is a powerful testimony to Luke's narrative skill that the reader is so caught up in the turbulent course of events that the difficulties are not immediately perceived. Archaeological and epigraphical evidence demonstrates the accuracy of his picture of the atmosphere in the city of Ephesus—we possess a body of Ephesian inscriptions which runs to ten volumes.[9]

---

[8] Suetonius, *Augustus*, 31, 3.
[9] Cf., e.g. P. Lampe, 'Acta 19 im Spiegel der ephesinischen Inschriften', *BZ* NF 36 (1992), 59–76; one may also consult W. Thiessen, *Christen in Ephesus: Die historische*

a. The goddess Artemis

In order to understand the narrative, some information about Artemis of Ephesus, her cult statue and temple is necessary. Researches have established that several deities were worshipped in Ephesus: Zeus, Aphrodite, Athene, Asclepius, Dionysus, Demeter and Hestia from the Greek pantheon, Serapis and Isis from Egypt, the Dea Roma from Rome, and divinised members of the imperial family as well as heroes from an earlier period. But the local goddess Artemis outshone all of these. She is known from Greek mythology as the virgin goddess of youth and of hunting, clad in a short tunic and armed with a bow. Sometimes, darker traits come to the foreground and she becomes a deity who brings death. Greek colonists in Asia Minor applied her name to a local mother goddess with similar characteristics, and carried out further assimilations. Nevertheless, the 'new' Artemis was not simply absorbed into the general mythology of the goddess: she remained an autonomous figure, Artemis of the Ephesians, venerated under this name in other places too. According to the local myth, she was born near the city. The welfare of the city was entrusted to her, and the people of Ephesus saw her as the divine protectress who preserved and cared for them.

Her cultic image is quite exceptional.[10] Its core is a smaller-than-life wooden figure, which had once been snatched from the fire and was blackened by age and by the oils with which it was anointed. It was clothed with garments and hung about with objects. In the course of time, further additions were made, such as a festal garment of hammered gold, necklaces with the signs of the zodiac, and a crenellated civic crown. It is only in the secondary reproductions of the original, i.e. the numerous stone statues of Artemis of Ephesus, that these ornaments merge with the basic figure to become one inseparable whole. This has important consequences for the most striking detail of the ornaments, which is especially prominent in the stone statues of Artemis, namely the rows of longish-round objects which cover the upper part of the goddess's body. Later Christian authors interpreted these as female breasts; they spoke of 'the many-breasted Artemis' and saw in her a fertility-goddess whose cult was suspected of including sexual orgies. But this interpretation is wrong for the simple reason that these round objects are not directly linked to the body of the original, but are hung on a breastplate before her; hence, they were detachable. We do not, however, know what these were; the identifications that have been proposed indicate more indirectly

---

und theologische Situation in vorpaulinischer und paulinischer Zeit und zur Zeit der Apostelgeschichte und der Pastoralbriefe (TANZ 12), Tübingen 1995, 90–110 (with further bibliography).

[10] Cf. R. Fleischer, Artemis von Ephesos und verwandte Kultstatuen aus Anatolien und Syrien (EPRO 35), Leiden 1973.

the aspect of fertility—eggs, dates, grapes, or the testicles of stallions which were sacrificed in the cult of Artemis.

The temple of Artemis lay somewhat outside the city, about two kilometres from the city centre in Roman times, and was counted among the seven wonders of the world. It covered an area of 130×70 metres. The Romans restricted, but did not abolish the sanctuary's right to grant asylum. Prayer texts were placed as inscriptions on its external walls. It was portrayed in stylised form on coins, and was added to the civic crown of the goddess in the time of Trajan. The temple had also great economic importance. It possessed lands and was allowed to receive bequests. Since it was regarded as impregnable on account of its sacred character, it also took on the function of a bank in which large sums of cash were deposited.

The temple was the focus of the two great annual festivals held in honour of the goddess, and of the monthly (if not indeed fortnightly) processions which went from the temple into the city and back again. The many visitors who came on these occasions led to the growth of a rich trade in pious souvenirs. According to our text (v. 24), miniature versions in silver of the temple of Artemis were produced and sold in large numbers. There may also have been silver shrines intended to hold small figures of Artemis, which would have been erected as sanctuaries in private houses, or silver amulets portraying the temple and the statue in relief. Up to now, however, only copies of the temple in terracotta and marble have been found, as well as miniature silver copies of the statue of Artemis, not silver temples or shrines. But while the reliability of this detail in Luke's account thus remains disputed, it does fit the general picture.

Demetrius was a popular name, found about sixty times in the Ephesian inscriptions. One Demetrius in the first century CE is even called *neopoios*, which however does not mean 'maker of temples' but rather 'guardian of the temple'—this could for example refer to a member of the administrative council. The inscriptions mention a silversmith and temple guardian with other names. Above all, they attest the existence of guilds of craftsmen. We encounter a cartel of fishermen and a guild of bakers, who actually cause a small riot and force the Roman proconsul to intervene.[11]

b. Demetrius' speech

A silversmith named Demetrius recognises the impending danger, and calls together the members of his guild and all those who worked in this sector of the economy as employees, suppliers, sellers, etc. (vv. 24f.). He delivers a short address which can at any rate claim the honour of

---

[11] Ephesian Inscriptions no. 215.

being honest. He makes no flimsy pretext of religious reasons, but comes directly to the point: this business is the basis of our financial well-being, but things can change if Paul has his way—this Paul who makes such an impact in Ephesus and in all Asia Minor with his assertion that gods whose images are made with human hands cannot be genuine gods (v. 26). Paul had in fact said something similar in his Areopagus speech (17:24, 29), and we need not repeat here what was said above about the history of the tradition of this critique of the gods in the Old Testament and in Judaism, and about the Epicurean and Stoic criticism of temples and public worship. We mention only in passing that Demetrius exaggerates, when he represents the progress of the Christian proclamation in Asia Minor at this early period as a success story; but this may well have edified Luke's intended readers.

Only after this introduction does Demetrius express his concern about 'the great goddess Artemis' (19:27). Things will go so far that her sanctuary will be despised 'and that she may even be deposed from her magnificence, she whom all Asia and the world worship'. This last remark refers not only to the many pilgrims who streamed to Ephesus from the Mediterranean world, but also to the expansion of the cult of Artemis of Ephesus, who had subordinate temples as far away as southern France and northern Africa. An inscription from Ephesus (no. 24 B 8–14) states:

> Since the goddess Artemis, who presides over our city, is venerated not only in her native territory, which she has made the most celebrated of all cities thanks to her own divinity, altars and temple precincts have been erected everywhere in her honour; sanctuaries have been built for her and altars erected to her because of the visible marvels that she has wrought.

The hearers pick up Demetrius' words about the 'great goddess' and her 'magnificence'. They fall into a rage and begin to shout, as with one voice: 'Great is Artemis of the Ephesians!' (v. 28). Other sources too, e.g. novels from the classical period and pagan inscriptions from Asia Minor referring to confession and atonement, refer likewise to the goddess Artemis, although they do not always employ liturgical acclamations coined explicitly for Ephesus, like this cry. One of these texts begins with the words: 'Great is Artemis Anaitis and Meis [Men] Tiamu.'[12] Jürgen Roloff comments on the acclamation by the crowd: 'Ultimately, this is nothing more than a desperate attempt to compensate for the brittleness of the religious-ideological basis by taking flight into intoxicating collective emotions.'[13]

---

[12] No. 69, 2f. in G. Petzl, *Die Beichtinschriften Westkleinasiens* (Epigraphica Anatolica 22), Bonn 1994, 88.
[13] J. Roloff, *Apg*, 292.

c. The tumult (vv. 29–34)

The silversmiths and their hangers-on succeed in provoking a general commotion in the city, and the populace rush to the one place capable of accommodating such a large crowd, viz. the theatre, which had a capacity of between twenty and twenty-six thousand places. This was where the regular assemblies were also held. A number of sources attest that tumults in cities began or culminated in the theatre. Flavius Josephus writes of a pogrom among the Jews that took place in Syrian Antioch during the Jewish War: one of the Jews 'appeared before the citizens of Antioch, who were gathered in the theatre', denounced his fellow Jews and also handed over 'some foreign Jews' who were accused of wanting to burn down the city.[14]

Two Macedonian travelling companions of Paul are immediately affected by the tumult. We know nothing else about Gaius, since he must be distinguished from Gaius of Derbe (Acts 20:4) and Gaius of Corinth (1 Cor 1:14); Aristarchus is better known from Philem 24 and Col 4:10. These two men are suddenly present in the theatre.

Although Paul himself has already been mentioned in Demetrius' speech, he does not feature in the narrative until v. 30: Paul does not want to leave his companions to their fate, but 'the disciples', i.e. members of the Ephesian Christian community, prevent him from entering the theatre. Verse 31 adds that 'Asiarchs' who were friends of Paul also sent word to him that he should avoid the theatre. 'Asiarch', literally 'leader of Asia', is an honorific title which apparently involved taking on representative duties for a period; it remained restricted to members of the small upper class. Although the title is attested in a number of inscriptions, we cannot say anything more precise about the activities of an Asiarch. Luke's intention is clear. Paul's message has reached members of the highest circles, who behave correctly (unlike the crowd, which has been whipped into a frenzy) and try to save Paul. In pragmatic terms, this also means that Luke portrays the support of philosophically educated and enlightened Gentiles: their world-view would lead such persons to a position of solidarity with the Christians, against fanatical busybodies in their own ranks.

It is difficult to say what lies historically behind this description of Paul's role. A number of passages in his letters indicate that he was in grave danger in Ephesus, e.g. the metaphor of fighting against beasts (1 Cor 15:32), Paul's despair when he no longer expects to survive (2 Cor 1:8–10), and the rescue by Prisca and Aquila, who risk their own necks for Paul in Ephesus (Rom 16:4). If these allusions are in fact connected to the Demetrius episode, then we must conclude that Luke has toned things down considerably and has kept Paul out of danger, since his *via*

---

[14] Flavius Josephus, *Bellum Judaicum* ('The Jewish War') 7, 46–62.

dolorosa is to be initiated only by means of an infuriated Jewish mob in Jerusalem; alternatively, Paul may not have featured at all in the tradition on which Luke drew, so that it was Luke himself who introduced him into the story, while consciously keeping him out of the epicentre.

Meanwhile, confusion breaks out in the theatre, and most of those present 'did not know why they had come together'. It is difficult to reconstruct what now follows in vv. 33f.; it almost seems as if the chaos described here is mirrored in the form of the text itself. Much depends on the translation of the first part, and the two most important possibilities can be summarised as follows.

(1) Most translators render v. 33: 'Some of the crowd prompted Alexander, when [or: because] the Jews put him forward [as their representative and spokesman].' When he comes to the front, Alexander raises his hand (a typical gesture for one who gives a speech) and wants to 'make a defence'. The crowd identify him as a Jew and prevent him from speaking, by shouting for two hours on end: 'Great is Artemis of the Ephesians!' From this perspective, Alexander's task is to defend the cause of Judaism. What is the reason for this? The turmoil has been unleashed by something that is an integral aspect of Judaism, viz. the criticism of statues of the gods. Paul was a Jew, and the Gentile populace of the city looked on the Christians as merely a more radical wing of Judaism, to the extent that they were capable of making any such differentiations at all. This is why the tumult threatens to turn into a pogrom of the Jews: the Jewish inhabitants of Ephesus are right to feel threatened. Their spokesman Alexander is to save the day for them, assuredly not by defending the companions of Paul, but rather by making clear to the enraged mob the difference between official Judaism and the new messianic sect.

(2) One can, however, also attempt to fill out the concise 'shorthand' introduction to v. 33 and translate it as follows:[15] 'They allowed Alexander [with whom you, the readers, are familiar] to come out of the crowd with [Gaius and Aristarchus], because the Jewish [Christians] pushed him forward.' The text speaks only of Jews, but this is because it adopts the perspective of the assembled crowd, who make no distinctions between Jews and Jewish Christians. The reality is that Alexander is to defend the Christian community, to which he belongs. The community will not abandon its companions in this hour of need, in which Paul himself is absent, and it does all it can to protect them. The crowd, however, know Alexander as a Jew and shout him down, because a latent anti-Judaism suddenly becomes virulent in this heated atmosphere. It would then seem possible to identify this Christian Alexander with Alexander the smith (!) in 1 Tim 1:20 and 2 Tim 4:14; the fact that

15 Cf. P. Lampe, 'Acts' (n. 9 above), 67.

Alexander appears in these texts as an opponent of Paul need not be an obstacle to this identification, since this may represent a subsequent development. In situations of great tribulation, even theological foes can demonstrate solidarity, something realised in exemplary fashion in this text.

Each type of solution has its own difficulties, but the second has the advantage of being more easily integrated into the tradition of Paul's letters. It is a pity that Alexander does not have the opportunity to make his defence, for his speech would have been a fine pendant to the accusations in Demetrius' speech and the deliberations in the town clerk's address. But Luke reserves discourses for Paul, not for his companions. The fact that the crowd shout out their acclamation of Artemis for two whole hours creates enough time, in the world of the narrative, to alert the authorities and compel them to come to the scene of events and take action.

d. The speech of the town clerk (vv. 35–40)

The town clerk, who appears in v. 35 and immediately calms things down, was the highest official in the Roman provincial administration. He displays diplomatic skill in his address, flattering the patriotic feelings of the crowds: everyone knows our city and is aware that it shelters the temple of the great Artemis and her image 'that fell from heaven'. 'Guardian of the temple' (neōkoros) was an official title bestowed on cities in Asia Minor which had a temple for the imperial cult; it seems that Ephesus was a special case, since the city was called 'guardian of the temple' of Artemis as early as the reign of Nero, before becoming a twofold 'guardian' when the imperial temple was established under Domitian. The heavenly origin of the image of Artemis is meant to make void the argument drawn from the criticism of religion in v. 26: Paul is wrong to assert that her statue was made with human hands. This idea may have its origin in meteorites that crashed into the earth and were venerated as fetishes. Euripides has Orestes address the following words to the god Apollo:

> And you bade me go to the land of the Taurians,
> to the altars of your sister Artemis,
> and to fetch from there the image of the gods which once
> fell down from heaven into this sanctuary.
> If I outfaced the danger and got hold of the image
> through guile and good luck, I was to bring it
> into the land of the Athenians. Your oracle said nothing further,
> only that this deed would bring healing to my madness.[16]

---

[16] Euripides, *Iphigeneia in Tauris*, 85–92; cf. 977f.

An appeal to keep calm follows in v. 36—one must 'do nothing rash'!—and then a declaration in v. 37 that Paul's companions are innocent: they are neither temple robbers, nor have they blasphemed our goddess. Theft from a temple, or desecration of a temple in general terms, was a grave crime. Flavius Josephus feels obliged to correct a malicious imputation against Judaism, which is based on a linguistic misunderstanding. The Greek word for theft from a temple is *hierosylia*, and we have seen above that the Greek name for Jerusalem is *Hierosolyma*. Enemies of Judaism assert that Jerusalem is a city of temple robbers, full of plundered goods.[17] Josephus rebuts this charge very decisively by citing the ordinance that 'no one is to revile the gods in whom foreign peoples believe; and it is forbidden to plunder foreign sanctuaries and to remove any image of a god from among the votive gifts'.[18] Political prudence can be detected in the surreptitious toning down of a text like Deut 7:25f. ('The graven images of their gods you shall burn with fire . . .'): it is better for a minority not to be too vigorous in attacking dominant religious paradigms. Rather, one should make a virtue of necessity and plead for a relative tolerance. Luke apparently wants to take a similar position here. The words of the town clerk apply to Christians, because while they do engage in the critique of religion, they are extremely careful to avoid every kind of violent action.

The town clerk next refers in vv. 38f. to the normal legal procedure, which envisages two authorities. A Roman proconsul held regular market days in the cities of his province, which were above all days for trying penal and capital cases. This would provide an opportunity for Demetrius and his guild to bring their accusation; but the text hints that they would be afraid to do so, since their accusations have too little substance. Besides this, there is the *ennomos ekklēsia*,[19] the legally-regulated assembly of the citizens of Ephesus. This body was competent to deal with religious questions connected with the practice of worship in the city, and the proconsul does not usually intervene here. The legal nature of this assembly is the antithesis of the tumultuous state of this 'unregulated' assembly in the theatre. One should note that we find here within the New Testament the concept of *ekklēsia*, with which we associate community and church, in its original political context. Perhaps we may go so far as to see a real 'anti-*ekklēsia*' in the disorderly gathering in the theatre, a caricature of what community assemblies are meant to be in the state and also in Christianity.

In v. 27, Demetrius conjured up the vision of a danger that threatened his business. A much greater danger is depicted in v. 40 by the town

---

[17] Flavius Josephus, *Contra Apionem* ('Against Apion') 1, 309–11.

[18] *Antiquitates Judaicae* ('Jewish Antiquities') 4, 207.

[19] Examples of this expression in Ephesus are: *Sylloge Inscriptionum Graecarum* (third edn) 672, 37f.; Ephesian Inscriptions 27, 54.

clerk: the proconsul could react with anger and demand that the populace of the city explain the reason for the riot and illegal assembly. This would have disagreeable consequences, and not only for the leaders of the mob: higher taxes, the loss of privileges and the removal of citizens' rights were only some of the penalties that could be inflicted. Dio Chrysostom speaks eloquently of this in his addresses to the cities of Asia Minor: 'For nothing that happens in the cities remains hidden from the pro-consuls. Just as children who behave badly at home are denounced by the family to the teachers, so too the misdemeanours of the towns are brought to the ears of the proconsuls' (*Or.* 46, 14). The town clerk of Ephesus has truly deserved the praise of a good counsellor which Dio Chrysostom makes in another passage (*Or.* 34, 33):

> I on the other hand affirm that a good counsellor, who deserves to be the head of a city, must in principle be armed against everything that people think burdensome, but especially against the abuse and rages of the mob. He must be like the foothills that cradle a harbour: all the might of the sea crashes against them, but within they keep the water in motionless stillness. He too must steel himself against the crowd; they may suddenly become angry and seek to abuse him. Here or in any other case, he must not let himself be affected by all their raging.

If we look at the narrative as a whole, we note that once again Luke unmasks Gentile religiosity, which in Demetrius' case is scarcely able to conceal economic interests. At the same time, he speaks in favour of a *modus vivendi*: he explicitly avoids recommending the blind rage that would attack the religious diversity in the milieu in which Christians live, for here he has some hope in the outcome of the free play of forces. Besides this, he indicates that Christians desire to be treated correctly by the authorities. They are not fair game for anyone, and they must not be exposed to the fluctuating moods of the mob. This expectation seems all the more justified, in that the Christians are on the side of the law: it is not they who cause riots, but rather their opponents. Finally, something akin to a situation of missionary competition comes into view here. Artemis of Ephesus has her devotees in all the Mediterranean world but Christianity is speedily catching up with her. Even Demetrius, the foe of Christianity, bears witness that it has already filled all Asia Minor.

VII

THE JOURNEY TO ROME (ACTS 27–28)

After the interlude of the silversmiths' riot, Paul sets out on his journey to Jerusalem, which he has already announced (Acts 19:21f.). All the time, however, the reader is aware of a horizon behind Judaism and Jerusalem. The first matter discussed in the meeting between Paul and James and the elders of the Jerusalem community is his activity among the Gentiles, which has given rise to misunderstandings (21:19f.). James recalls the apostolic decree with the clauses he had proposed (21:25). At vv. 27–29, Jews from Asia Minor stir up a tumult against Paul, similar to the riot in Ephesus: they suspect him of having broken the law by bringing a Gentile Christian from Ephesus into the inner court of the temple (cf. the echoes of this accusation at 24:6 and 25:8). When he relates the experience of his vocation in direct speech before Felix, he tells of an additional vision in which he was charged to preach to the Gentile peoples (22:21), and his account before Agrippa II speaks in greater detail on the same subject (26:17–23).

The following chapters, up to Acts 26, concentrate on Jerusalem and Caesarea. Their main contents are the complications of religious and power politics in which Paul becomes entangled, and the various stages of his judicial trial, which cannot be brought to a completion in Palestine. We never lose sight of the orientation to Rome which is laid down at 19:21. The Lord appears to Paul by night and assures him that he will bear witness as far as Rome (23:11); and when Paul draws attention to his rights as a Roman citizen (22:25–29) and then appeals to the emperor in Rome (25:11f.), he succeeds in fulfilling this charge to maintain the momentum of his journey to Rome. According to Agrippa II, it is only this appeal that prevents the trial from ending in Caesarea with acquittal for Paul (26:32). Festus, the governor, uses the honorific name Sebastos, i.e. Augustus, for the emperor at 25:25.

1. *Sea voyage, shipwreck, rescue (Acts 27:1–44)*

The continuation of the trial in Rome makes a journey necessary, and Luke devotes ch. 27 to the account of this sea voyage. Dramatic descriptions of sea voyages, with storms, wanderings, shipwrecks and miraculous rescues, are an established part of the repertoire of epic narrative literature in antiquity, from Homer's *Odyssey* to the romantic novels of the imperial period. But it is not this comparison that interests us here; rather, we wish to investigate what Acts 27 indicates about our general theme.[1]

At 27:3, we are told that the Roman centurion Julius, who is in charge of the transport, acts *philanthrōpōs*, 'kindly'. Later, when he prevents the soldiers from killing the prisoners (v. 43), his kindness helps ensure that all are rescued.

An angel of God assures Paul by night that God still wishes to lead him to Rome, into the presence of the emperor (v. 24). This is why God will also rescue all his travelling companions. Verse 26 already notes that they will run aground on an island, as then happens at 28:1.

Paul encourages his companions by telling them about this heavenly assurance. His first words are: 'An angel of the God to whom I belong . . .' (v. 23). The fact that the majority of the two hundred and seventy-six persons on board (v. 37) are Gentiles makes it necessary to specify this; the story is related from the perspective of the Christian 'we'-group, who accompany Paul, but these were few in number (cf. the mention of Aristarchus in v. 2). When the total number is given in v. 37, however, this 'we' becomes what Karl Löning has called a 'we of the community in trouble': 'We were in all two hundred and seventy-six persons in the ship.' No one is allowed to break out of this fellowship, neither the crew, who plan to escape by stealth (vv. 30–32), nor the soldiers, who are tempted to take desperate action (v. 42). The rescue will succeed only if all stay together.

In v. 34, Paul repeats in his own words what the angel of God has told him: 'Not a hair is to perish from the head of any of you.' Jesus had said this in the Gospel to the persecuted disciples (Lk 21:18), but here it is extended to the very mixed company of persons on board the ship.

Paul then takes bread (vv. 35f.), utters the prayer of thanksgiving, breaks the bread and begins to eat. Serious objections are often made to the idea that he celebrates the eucharist 'on the waves of the Mediter-ranean':[2] surely Paul cannot share the eucharist with pagans? Nor can he celebrate it for himself alone, since it is a meal and hence is orientated towards fellowship. The conclusion drawn is that we must exclude all eucharistic associations. Against this we have the very decided evidence of the actual words Luke uses. An intermediary solution would be that Paul celebrates a eucharistic meal, perhaps only with the immediate circle of his Christian companions; his fellow travellers imitate him by taking nourishment and so regain their strength. Thus they too share in the blessing which comes from the celebration. It is not only here that rescue from distress at sea becomes a transparent image for the rescue and salvation of the human person in general.

[1] On what follows, cf. R. C. Tannehill, *Narrative Unity*, 330–43; K. Löning, 'Gottesbild', 89–92.

[2] Cf. B. Reicke, 'Die Mahlzeit mit Paulus auf den Wellen des Mittelmeers. Act. 27, 33–38', *ThZ* 4 (1948), 401–10.

Pagans are drawn here in a very significant manner into the Christian experience of salvation. The only condition for this is the renunciation of all egotistic behaviour, and the first basic requirement is a humane ethos ('kindness'). This does not exclude the exhortation to repent and turn to the true God, but other matters are more pressing here. We begin to see the contours of the possibility of a preliminary inclusive experience of salvation.

2. The hospitable island (Acts 28:1–10)

The 'we'-form in 28:1–2, 7, 10 continues the narrative of the sea voyage. Three short miracle stories are inserted into these verses: Paul is unharmed by a snake bite (vv. 3–6), he heals the father of Publius, who has a fever (v. 8), and a summary speaks of other healings (v. 9). An inherent connection is provided by the idea that the one who was rescued from distress at sea now proves in turn to be one who rescues others.

a. The wonder-worker at the camp fire (vv. 1–6)[3]

We do not wish to discuss recent scholarly debate about the localisation of the island of *Melitē*, which is surely identical with Malta. The narrative structure brings us to an outpost of the inhabited world, among barbarians with rough manners and a foreign language. One can imagine the inhabitants of the island reacting in various ways, and classical novels do in fact depict such figures as pirates waiting on the shore and cannibals; but nothing of that kind happens here. The natives display an extreme friendliness, and this is all the more significant when we recall that *philanthrōpia* was seen as the virtue of rulers and kings. In concrete terms, the inhabitants of the island show this kindness when they light a great fire for the drenched and freezing victims of the shipwreck.

Paul too wishes to make himself useful, not only to be served, but also to serve (cf. Lk 22:27) with his own hands (cf. Acts 20:34). He gathers firewood, but while he is throwing it into the fire, a poisonous snake shoots out of a bundle of twigs and bites his hand. It can be objected here that there are no poisonous snakes on Malta, but this would ignore completely the laws of the narrative world, especially in view of similar scenes in epics and myths. We need only recall Philoctetes, one of the heroes in the Greek army, who is bitten by a snake on an island *en route* for Troy. Since the suppurating wound refuses to heal and causes a terrible stench, he is put ashore on another island. Later he is healed and rejoins the army.[4]

---

[3] Cf. G. Schille, *Apg*, 470; S. Schreiber, *Paulus als Wundertäter*, 122–37.
[4] Cf. Homer, *Iliad*, 2, 718ff.; Sophocles, *Philoctetes*, 254–74; and many other texts.

The barbarians who see this reflect upon it in v. 4. Their first wrong evaluation is that Paul must be a murderer, or even worse. His shipwreck on its own could be interpreted as a punishment for evil deeds which had neither been expiated nor avenged; he has been rescued from the sea, but Dikē, the goddess of justice, does not relax her grip on him—she sends the poisonous snake, which is to finish her work. An epigram which is quoted in commentaries on Acts as a parallel text describes the sequence of shipwreck, rescue and death by a snake bite, not as a punishment, but as an illustration of the inscrutability and inescapable character of destiny:

> Once, when a broken-down man had escaped from the storm and fury
> of the cruel sea, he lay not far from the swell of the sea,
> naked on the Libyan sand. Dull sleep lay heavy upon him,
> since the distress of shipwreck had exhausted his strength,
> when the poisonous viper bit him . . . So he had wrestled with the waves,
> only to meet on land the death that was decreed for him.[5]

Another epigram in fact comes even closer. It speaks, not of a snake, but of the deadly bite of a seal, and sees this death as the penalty for an attempted murder in the struggle to get hold of a plank that would save the man from the sea:

> A ship broke apart on the sea with a crash. Two men fought
> over a plank, since only one was available to the disputants.
> And Antagoras smote Peisistratos. Can one reproach him for this?
> Was not his life in danger? Yet punishment did not sleep:
> Peisistratos saved his life by swimming away,
> but a seal took hold of Antagoras.
> The fates exercise their office of vengeance even on the high seas.[6]

The reader already knows that the hypothesis put forward in v. 5 is invalid, since Paul is guarded by the assurance in the logion of Jesus in Lk 10:19, 'Behold, I have given you power to tread upon serpents and scorpions', which will do no harm (cf. Mk 16:18). This means that nothing serious can happen to him before he has reached the goal of his journey, Rome. This is a narrative of a miracle of punishment and rescue, and it would be completely beside the point to speculate whether perhaps Paul was immune to snake poison, or whether the snake was in fact not poisonous at all.

Paul shakes the snake off into the fire, but the barbarians sit down and look expectantly at him—when will he swell up and drop dead? Some time goes by, but nothing happens. Now they change their opinion and tell each other that Paul is surely a god (v. 6). This is their second wrong

[5] *Anthologia Graeca*, 7.290 (Statilius Flaccus).
[6] Idem 9.269 (Antipatros of Thessalonica).

evaluation. When we compare it with what happened in Lystra, this reaction seems almost harmless, since no preparations are made to offer sacrifice. Nevertheless, it is suprising that the narrative simply goes on, and that (unlike in Lystra) this evaluation is not put right. Has everything necessary already been said in Lystra, so that there is no longer any danger of misunderstandings? Is the reader meant to infer from the first wrong evaluation that the second is likewise incorrect? Or does Luke wish here to offer a positive portrait of the barbarians, whose kindness makes them open to the divine working?

b. A beginning reminiscent of the times of Jesus (vv. 7–10)

Jesus begins his miraculous activity in Luke's Gospel by healing Peter's mother-in-law of fever and then restoring health to many sick persons by the laying-on of his hands (Lk 4:38–40). It is impossible to overlook the parallels in Acts 28:8–9. But first we meet a nobleman with the Roman name Publius (v. 7), who exercises a kind of presidential office as 'the chief man of the island' and possesses large estates. He is no less friendly (*philophronōs*) than Julius and the barbarians: he takes the shipwrecked men into his home for three whole days, with exemplary hospitality. He does this without any ulterior motive: it is only in the next verse that we hear of the illness of his father. Once again, Luke has the opportunity to show Paul in the company of representatives of a Romanised upper class.

The father of Publius lies in bed, racked with fever and diarrhoea, and Paul heals him with prayer and the laying-on of hands (v. 8). This combination of prayer and the laying-on of hands within the account of a healing miracle is unparalleled. The laying-on of hands can be understood as the communication of power, or else simply as an expression of care. Paul's prayer is addressed to God and supplies an answer, within the text itself, to v. 6: Paul is no god, but merely a messenger who carries out God's commands. He has himself received good things, and now he repays this in kind by doing good to Publius' father.

The one healing leads to many healings in v. 9. It seems that all the sick inhabitants of the island come or are brought to Paul, who heals them all. There are no exorcisms (unlike in Lk 4:41), but these do not play the same role in Acts in general as in the Gospel. For Luke, they are a sign of the period of Jesus rather than of the apostolic period; one reason for this may be that they are more exposed to the suspicion of magic than the healings.

The bestowing of benefits in return for honours was a transaction that functioned admirably in the classical world. In v. 10, the inhabitants pay fitting honour to Paul, the saviour of the island. We are not told exactly what happened. The usual forms were garlands, inscriptions and statues, but this would be much too close to what happened at Lystra. Besides this, the natives provide a generous supply of food and equipment for the group of travellers, when they depart after spending three months on the island. They do not cling fearfully to their possessions, but are happy to share them wherever they see people in need.

c. Under the sign of the Dioscuri (v. 11)

Paul and his companions continue their journey on an Alexandrian ship that had wintered in the island. This ship bore the sign of the Dioscuri. Although three-dimensional statues of the gods were sometimes carried on ships as protective deities, this particular sign was not a carved wooden figurehead, but an image of the Dioscuri painted on both the external walls of the ship and inscribed with their names.[7] As their name indicates, the Dioscuri were sons of Zeus; they are most commonly interpreted as the divine brothers Castor and Pollux, who were invoked as gods of rescue. Their speciality was rescue from distress at sea, so that they were also patrons of sea voyages. In an account of a sea voyage in Lucian, 'one of the Dioscuri, in the form of a brightly shining star, takes his place aloft on the mast, on the cross-beam, and steers the ship which was already making for the rocks, so that it takes a course to port, reaching the high seas in the nick of time'.[8] A rationalistic explanation can compare the Dioscuri with a constellation of twin stars that appears in the sky when the clouds suddenly break after a violent storm (St Elmo's fire has also been suggested). The Homeric hymn addressed to them transposes their activity into the realm of myth:

> They became saviours of those on earth and saviours of the swift ships.
> When hurricanes rear their heads in the inexorable sea,
> the sailors call with prayers on the sons of mighty Zeus
> and rush to the bow of the deck to sacrifice white lambs.
> The ship is already pressed down deep into the water by the great wind,
> by the waves of the sea, when suddenly—what a sight!—they sweep
> downwards from the sky on pale wings,
> at once banishing the confusion of the terrible winds and spreading
> smoothness out over the sea as the bright salty spume flows:
> good omens for the sailors, that their endeavours are not in vain.
> They rejoice at the sight, for their woe and struggle are ended.[9]

What does it mean when Paul boards such a ship? One is almost inclined to suggest that the earlier misadventure will not be repeated with this ship, which enjoys special protection. It will bring Paul safely and without danger to Italy. Does God then make use of foreign troops? But this idea

---

[7] Cf. F. J. Dölger, '"Dioskuroi". Das Reiseschiff des Apostels Paulus und seine Schutzgötter. Kult- und Kulturgeschichtliches zu *Apg* 28, 11', *AuC* 6 (1950), 276–85.

[8] Lucian, *Navigium* ('The Ship') 9.

[9] Homeric Hymns 33: 'To the Dioscuri' 6–17.

surely goes too far, even for Luke. At any rate, we see no evidence of any blind fanaticism or religious intransigence on Paul's part. He is not disturbed by these external forms of pagan worship of the gods, but uses the things he needs.

Such pagans, who behave so kindly and nobly as the Roman centurion Julius, the barbarians on Malta, and Publius with his large estates, are (so to speak) predestined for salvation in the Christian sense of the word. Unlike Cornelius in Caesarea, they are not numbered among the 'God-fearers', since they have not come into contact with the mediating work of Judaism; on the other hand, it is also true that a great gulf separates them from the unenlightened crowd in Lystra. The Christian hope of salvation reaches here across borders that certainly do not go unnoticed. This hope allows persons of very various origins and life experiences to share in salvation, even when there is no immediate missionary success and conversion. Virtues such as hospitality and generosity retain their value, even when practised by non-Christians.

3. *Freedom to preach in Rome (Acts 28:16–31)*[10]

The concluding section, speaking of Paul's arrival and residence in Rome, notes once again that after Israel's refusal, which is displayed by the Jews of Rome in part (cf. vv. 21f.: their reaction is mixed), God's message of salvation takes the path to the Gentile peoples, who receive it with joy (cf. Acts 13:45–49). Not only does the precise formulation in v. 28, that 'this salvation (*sōtērion*) of God has been sent to the Gentiles', evoke Is 40:5 LXX ('And all flesh shall see the salvation of God') and Acts 13:26 ('To us has been sent the message of this salvation (*sōtēria*)'); it also creates a link back to the beginning of the Gospel, since Lk 3:6 quotes Is 40:3–5, while old Simeon has earlier seen the child Jesus in the temple at Jerusalem and formulated the prophecy: 'My eyes have seen your salvation, which you have prepared in the presence of all peoples, a light for revelation to the Gentiles, and for glory to your people Israel' (Lk 2:30–32).

The final section poses the difficult question of what Luke's final words are on the relation of the Christian Church to God's people Israel and on the role of the Jewish people in salvation history. For example, does he one-sidedly alter the dual aspect of Simeon's prophecy—revelation to the Gentiles and glory to Israel—in favour of the Gentiles? A more detailed discussion of this issue would go beyond the framework of our subject, and require a new book of its own. Let us be content with the following indication: it is often maintained that the close of the Acts of

---

[10] H. J. Hauser, *Strukturen der Abschlusserzählung der Apostelgeschichte (Apg 28, 16–31)* (AnBib 86), Rome 1979, here 43. The book deals with the closing narrative as a whole.

the Apostles propagates a definitive solution to the challenge which Judaism poses to the consciousness of Christian identity, but this is quite wrong. In many ways, the end of Acts is given an open form, and one aspect of this openness is the fact that the question of Israel does not find any real answer, but remains a mystery. Even within the context of Isaiah, the accusation of hardness of heart (6:9f., quoted at Acts 28:26f.) is not the final word, but only marks one stage in God's history with his people— a history that is full of tension and often tragic.

The two final verses (28:30f.) stand somewhat on their own. Paul spends two years in rented lodgings, where he receives all who wish to visit him (v. 30), Jews and Gentiles, although these are individuals, no longer groups. One should not overlook the painful restriction on the apostle's activity entailed by his custody, the uncertain continuation and outcome of his trial, and the opposition of many of the Roman Jews. But instead of being downcast, he defends the main points of the Christian proclamation to those who visit him: he speaks of the kingdom of God and presents the doctrine concerning the Lord Jesus Christ. In other words, he interprets the Jesus-event as the fulfilment of the promises of God recorded in the Old Testament, and he does so 'quite openly and un-hindered' (v. 31). Free and courageous speech, refusing to bow to any intimidation, was defended in the Athenian democracy as an ideal against all tyrants. This is the term applied to the courageous behaviour of the apostle: the final word of Acts, 'unhindered', is an adverb describing not his personal situation, but his preaching. In other words, the intention is not to say that the light conditions of imprisonment, with a soldier guarding him (v. 16), are no great hindrance for Paul. Rather, Luke wishes to show that even external conditions of hardship cannot fetter the word of God (cf. 2 Tim 2:9). It sweeps aside all obstacles, thanks to the power which dwells within it.

The programme outlined in Acts 1:8, crossing all boundaries and aiming at the ends of the earth, is not yet fulfilled when Paul reaches Rome. But this is a movement which presses vigorously ahead. Not even Rome will bring it to a stop; nor does it depend on the person of Paul alone. Its nature is defined in the text itself, which—with 'unhindered' as its final word—points beyond itself into a future that lies open.

VIII

RETROSPECT AND PROSPECT

The concentration on one specific topic always risks giving exaggerated importance to those elements which are relevant to one's theme and leaving out of consideration other perspectives which are in fact no less important. We may begin by conceding that the confrontation with magic and the Gentiles is not the only concern, nor indeed even the chief concern, of the Acts of the Apostles; for example, the definition of the relationship to Judaism is much more urgent in Luke's eyes. Nor does Acts offer a complete description of the polytheistic system or of the practice of magic which would make possible a more penetrating theoretical discussion. This would not be in keeping with the narrative character of the book. Instead, Acts employs dramatic episodes, verbal discourses, summary descriptions of the state of affairs, and narrative commentaries.

If one assembles these individual fragments, the result is a very broad and vivid picture. In the course of the narrative, we gradually encounter a whole series of contemporary religious phenomena, each represented by specific adherents: magicians, astrologers and exorcists of Jewish or semi-Jewish provenance; a king who does not distance himself sufficiently from the cult of rulers, in an episode which also addresses the Roman imperial cult; a seer on a small scale, with her greedy owners, as exponent of the classical *manteia*; devotees of polytheistic belief, who have recourse to familiar forms of sacrifice, or who defend the goddess of their city and fear for the future of their traffic in devotional souvenirs; philosophers whose curiosity is more noticeable than their academic training; but also kindly barbarians and some genuinely 'noble' pagans.

Despite all the criticism of some defective forms, we do not find any heavily aggressive polemic. Instead, there is a subtle irony which occasionally takes the form of brilliant parodies. Simon Magus and Bar-Jesus are the objects of the fiercest attacks, and the severest punishment falls on Herod Agrippa I. In the case of the hapless exorcists in Ephesus, laughter is the appropriate reaction, while we feel real compassion for the poor slave-girl in Philippi who proves to be a Gentile prophetess. The concluding passage attributes a humane ethos even to barbarians and Romans, although there is nothing to indicate their conversion to Christianity. The God-fearers have earlier been depicted in this light. It follows that Luke cannot have had a very negative view of the human race. In keeping with this refusal to launch direct attacks, he continuously strives to portray the Christian proclamation as politically harmless: where it is tolerated, it is aware of its obligation to be loyal to the state.

In shaping his narrative sequence, Luke must distance his own protagonists, with their striking miracles—even involving handkerchiefs, in the case of Paul—from magicians like Simon or Bar-Jesus. This is no easy task, since outward appearances are very similar. Luke develops a variety of strategies: he orientates and subordinates the miracles of the Christian messengers to the proclamation of the word; he also attempts to the best of his ability, on the basis of the biblical faith in creation, to exclude every confusion between God and human beings and every transgression of the boundary between the divine and the human spheres— a danger that was constantly present in concepts such as that of the 'divine human being'. His heroes always point to the power working in them, a power not their own, something that they do not possess as individuals; they reject any cult of persons. Money is a very sensitive subject for Luke. The Christian preachers refuse any payment, and the desire of their opponents to make a profit by combining religion and business is a universal weapon which he employs to discredit a number of forms of pagan religiosity; this also entails a corresponding obligation on his own communities and their office-bearers. His fundamentally eirenic attitude is seen once again, when he partly goes along with the pagan critique of religion: it ought to be possible to agree with enlightened pagans that temples, statues, and the usual cultic practices are unworthy of a faith that has been the object of philosophical reflection.

This already brings us on to a meta-level which lies beyond the narrative sequence. What Luke aims to bring about in his readers is not necessarily identical with what he presents in his narrative. Thus, he surely did not conceive of the Areopagus discourse as an exemplary sermon to Gentiles in his own historical period: rather, he wants to use it to convince his readers that they need not be ashamed of their Christian faith before the forum of reason. After conversion has taken place, one can certainly look back and justify faith on rational terms, since it translates a dim perception in the human soul into a clear decision, and faith is capable of adopting the best traditions of the philosophical criticism of religion. The open conclusion of many episodes aims likewise at the age in which the readers live. This makes it clear that Luke fears above all the survival of remnants of popular religiosity in his communities, and that he does not regard his Christians as secure from occasional lapses into magical practices. We can take an example from our own time, in order to make clear the problems involved here: may a believing Christian order the course of his or her day on the basis of the horoscope in the daily tabloid newspaper? Luke would surely have had grave objections to this, and he would have found a suitable story to illustrate the question.

We must read all the individual episodes anew from this reader-orientated perspective, for they open up afresh every aspect of the confrontation with pagan forms of religion. The text portrays this confrontation as something that occurred in the past. Today's problems are often different, and they must be resolved in an analogous manner. But if we concentrate in this way on the Christian background, have we not quietly ditched the missionary perspective—a perspective which this book has attempted to follow through the whole of Acts, from the first chapter to the last? Not necessarily, and not entirely. The primary intention of the Acts of the Apostles as a book is not missionary, but it does portray missionary history, as an inspiration to the reader. The model stories within the narrative help to form and stabilise the identity of the Christian readers. Luke's correct intuition here is that only a community that enjoys internal stability will be able to manage the difficult balancing act which is continually demanded between seeking contact and offering contradiction, between the search for common elements and the endeavour to identify boundaries, i.e. between inculturation and evangelisation.

BIBLIOGRAPHY

1. *Commentaries on Acts of the Apostles*

BARRETT, C. K. *A Critical and Exegetical Commentary on the Acts of the Apostles,* vol. 1–2. International Critical Commentary. Edinburgh: T&T Clark, 1994–98.

CONZELMANN, HANS. *Acts of the Apostles.* Translated by James Limburg et al. Hermeneia. Philadelphia: Fortress Press, 1987. German rev. ed. 1972.

DUNN, JAMES D. G. *The Acts of the Apostles.* Epworth Commentaries. Peterborough: Epworth, 1996.

ECKEY, WILFRIED. *Die Apostelgeschichte: Der Weg des Evangeliums von Jerusalem nach Rom.* 2 vols. Neukirchen-Vluyn: Neukirchener, 2000.

FITZMYER, JOSEPH A. *The Acts of the Apostles.* Anchor Bible 31. New York: Doubleday, 1998.

HAENCHEN, ERNST. *The Acts of the Apostles: A Commentary.* Translated by Bernard Noble and Gerald Shinn. Edited by R. McL. Wilson. Philadelphia: Westminster, 1971. 16th German ed. 1977.

JERVELL. JACOB. *Die Apostelgeschichte.* Kritisch-exegetischer Kommentar über das Neue Testament 3. Göttingen: Vandenhoeck & Ruprecht, 1998. (See review by Klauck, *Biblische Zeitschrift* 43 [1999] 142–43.)

JOHNSON, LUKE TIMOTHY. *The Acts of the Apostles.* Sacra Pagina 5. Collegeville, Minn.: Liturgical, 1992.

KEE, HOWARD CLARK. *To Every Nation under Heaven: The Acts of the Apostles.* New Testament in Context. Harrisburg, Pa.: Trinity, 1997.

LÜDEMANN, GERD. *Early Christianity according to the Traditions in Acts: A Commentary.* Translated by John Bowden. Minneapolis: Fortress Press, 1989. German ed. 1987.

MUSSNER, FRANZ. *Die Apostelgeschichte.* Neue Echter Bible: Kommentar zum Neuen Testament 5. Würzburg: Echter, 1984.

PESCH, RUDOLF. *Die Apostelgeschichte.* 2 vols. Evangelisch-katholischer Kommentar zum Neuen Testament 5. Zurich: Benziger; Neukirchen-Vluyn: Neukirchener, 1986.

ROLOFF, JÜRGEN. *Die Apostelgeschichte.* Neue Testament Deutsch 5. Göttingen: Vandenhoeck & Ruprecht, 1981.

SCHILLE, GOTTFRIED. *Die Apostelgeschichte des Lukas.* Theologischer Handkommentar zum Neuen Testament 5. Berlin: Evangelische Verlaganstalt, 1983.

SCHMITHALS, WALTER. *Die Apostelgeschichte des Lukas.* Zürcher Bibelkommentar. Neues Testament 3.2. Zurich: Theologischer Verlag, 1982.

SCHNEIDER, GERHARD. *Die Apostelgeschichte.* 2 vols. Herders theologischer Kommentar zum Neuen Testament 5. Freiburg: Herder, 1980–82.

SPENCER, F. SCOTT. *Acts.* Readings. Sheffield: Sheffield Academic, 1997.

WEISER, ALFONS. *Die Apostelgeschichte.* 2 vols. Ökumenischer Taschenbuchkommentar zum Neuen Testament 5/1-2. Gütersloh: Gütersloher; Würzburg: Echter, 1981, 1985.

WITHERINGTON, BEN III. *The Acts of the Apostles: A Socio-Rhetorical Commentary.* Grand Rapids: Eerdmans, 1998.

ZAHN, THEODOR. *Die Apostelgeschichte des Lukas.* 2 vols. Kommentar zum Neuen Testament 5/1–2. Leipzig: Deichert, 1919–21.

ZMIJEWSKI, JOSEF. *Die Apostelgeschichte.* Regensburger Neues Testament. Regensburg: Pustet, 1994.

2. Monographs and Articles on Acts

ARLANDSON, JAMES MALCOLM. *Women, Class, and Society in Early Christianity: Models from Luke–Acts.* Peabody, Mass.: Hendrickson, 1997.

AVEMARIE, FRIEDRICH. *Die Tauferzählungen der Apostelgeschichte: Theologie und Geschichte.* Wissenschaftliche Untersuchungen zum Neuen Testament 139. Tübingen: Mohr/Siebeck, 2002.

BARTCHY, S. SCOTT. 'Community of Goods in Acts: Idealization or Social Reality?' In *The Future of Early Christianity: Essays in Honor of Helmut Koester,* edited by Birger A. Pearson, 309–18. Minneapolis: Fortress Press, 1991.

BEUTLER, JOHANNES. 'Die paulinische Heidenmission am Vorabend des Apostelkonzils.' *Theologie und Philosophie* 43 (1968) 360–83.

BONZ, MARIANNE PALMER. *The Past as Legacy: Luke–Acts and Ancient Epic.* Minneapolis: Fortress Press, 2000.

BOSSUYT, PHILIPPE, and JEAN RADERMAKERS. *Témoins de la Parole de la Grâce: Actes des Aptres.* 2 vols. Collection Institut d'études théologiques 16. Brussels: Institut d'etudes theologiques, 1995.

BRAWLEY, ROBERT L. *Centering on God: Method and Message in Luke–Acts.* Literary Currents in Biblical Interpretation. Louisville: Westminster John Knox, 1990.

CASSIDY, RICHARD J. *Society and Politics in the Acts of the Apostles.* Maryknoll, N.Y.: Orbis, 1987.

———, and PHILIP J. SCHARPER, editors. *Political Issues in Luke–Acts.* Maryknoll, N.Y.: Orbis, 1983.

DIBELIUS, MARTIN. *Studies in the Acts of the Apostles*. Edited by Heinrich Greeven. Translated by Mary Ling. London: SCM, 1956. 4th German ed. 1961.

DOWNING, F. GERALD. 'Common Ground with Paganism in Luke and in Josephus.' *New Testament Studies* 28 (1982) 546–59.

DUPONT, JACQUES. *Études sur les Actes des Apôtres*. Lectio Divina 45. Paris: Cerf, 1967.

———. *The Salvation of the Gentiles: Essays on the Acts of the Apostles*. Translated by John R. Keating. New York: Paulist, 1979. (Selections from the essays in the 1967 volume.)

ELLIGER, WINFRIED. *Paulus in Griechenland: Philippi, Thessaloniki, Athen, Korinth*. 2d ed. Stuttgarter Bibelstudien 92/93. Stuttgart: Katholisches Bibelwerk, 1990.

ESLER, PHILIP F. *Community and Gospel in Luke–Acts: The Social and Political Motivations of Lucan Theology*. Society for New Testament Studies Monograph Series 57. Cambridge: Cambridge Univ. Press, 1987

FLETCHER-LOUIS, CRISPIN T. H. *Luke–Acts: Angels, Christology, and Soteriology*. Wissenschaftliche Untersuchungen zum Neuen Testament 2/94. Tübingen: Mohr/Siebeck, 1997.

FOAKES-JACKSON, F. J., and KIRSOPP LAKE, editors. *The Beginnings of Christianity: Acts of the Apostles*. 5 vols. London: Macmillan, 1919–33.

GARRETT, SUSAN R. *The Demise of the Devil: Magic and the Demonic in Luke's Writings*. Minneapolis: Fortress Press, 1989.

GRÄSSER, ERICH. *Forschungen zur Apostelgeschichte*. Wissenschaftliche Untersuchungen zum Neuen Testament 137. Tübingen: Mohr/Siebeck, 2001.

HEDRICK, CHARLES W. 'Paul's Conversion/Call: A Comparative Analysis of the Three Reports in Acts.' *Journal of Biblical Literature* 100 (1981) 415–32.

HEMER, COLIN J. *The Book of Acts in the Setting of Hellenistic History*. Wissenschaftliche Untersuchungen zum Neuen Testament 49. Tübingen: Mohr/Siebeck, 1989.

HILL, CRAIG C. *Hellenists and Hebrews: Reappraising Division within the Earliest Church*. Minneapolis: Fortress Press, 1992.

HORN, FRIEDRICH WILHELM, editor. *Das Ende des Paulus: Historische, theologische und literaturgeschichtliche Aspekte*. Beihefte zur Zeitschrift für die neutestamentliche Wissenschaft 106. Berlin: de Gruyter, 2001.

JERVELL, JACOB. *The Unknown Paul: Essays on Luke–Acts and Early Christian History*. Minneapolis: Augsburg, 1984.

JOHNSON, LUKE TIMOTHY. *Sharing Possessions: Mandate and Symbol of Faith*. Overtures to Biblical Theology. Philadelphia: Fortress Press, 1981.

KECK, LEANDER E., and J. LOUIS MARTYN, editors. *Studies in Luke–Acts*. Philadelphia: Fortress Press, 1980 [1966].

KEE, HOWARD CLARK. *Good News to the Ends of the Earth: The Theology of Acts*. Philadelphia: Trinity, 1990.

KLAUCK, HANS-JOSEF. 'With Paul in Paphos and Lystra: Magic and Paganism in the Acts of the Apostles.' *Neotestamentica* 28 (1994) 93–108.

KLEIN, GÜNTER. 'Der Synkretismus als theologisches Problem in der ältesten christlichen Apologetik.' *Zeitschrift für Theologie und Kirche* 64 (1967) 40–82. Reprinted in Klein, *Rekonstruktion und Interpretation: Gesammelte Aufsätze zum Neuen Testament*, 262–301. Beiträge zur evangelische Theologie 50. Munich: Kaiser, 1969.

KORN, MANFRED. *Die Geschichte Jesu in veränderter Zeit: Studien zur bleibenden Bedeutung Jesu im lukanischen Doppelwerk*. Wissenschaftliche Untersuchungen zum Neuen Testament 2/51. Tübingen: Mohr/Siebeck, 1993.

KREMER, JACOB, editor. *Les Actes des Apôtres: Traditions, Rédaction, Théologie*. Bibliotheca Ephemeridum Theologicarum Lovaniensium 48. Gembloux: Duculot, 1979.

LIN, SZU-CHUAN. *Wundertaten und Mission: Dramatische Episoden in Apg 13–14*. Europäische Hochschulschriften 23/623. Frankfurt: Lang, 1998.

LÖNING, KARL. 'Das Evangelium und die Kulturen: Heilsgeschichtliche und kulturelle Aspekte kirchlicher Realität in der Apostelgeschichte.' In *Aufstieg und Niedergang der römischen Welt* 2.25.3 (1985) 2604–46.

———. 'Das Gottesbild der Apostelgeschichte im Spannungsfeld von Frühjudentum und Fremdreligion.' In *Monotheismus und Christologie: Zur Gottesfrage im hellenistischen Judentum und im Urchristentum*, edited by Hans-Josef Klauck, 88–117. Quaestiones disputatae 138. Freiburg: Herder, 1992.

MADDOX, ROBERT. *The Purpose of Luke–Acts*. Forschungen zur Religion und Literatur des Alten und Neuen Testaments 126. Göttingen: Vandenhoeck & Ruprecht, 1982.

MARGUERAT, DANIEL. 'Magie, guérison et parole dans les Actes des apôtres.' *Etudes Théologiques et Religigieuses* 72 (1997) 197–208. Revised edition in Marguerat, *La première Histoire du Christianisme: Les Actes des apôtres*, 175–203. Lectio Divina 180. Paris: Cerf, 1999.

———. *The First Christian Historian: Acts of the Apostles*. Translated by Ken McKinney et al. Society for New Testament Studies Monograph Series 121. Cambridge: Cambridge Univ. Press, 2002. French ed. 1999.

MARSHALL, I. HOWARD, and DAVID PETERSON. *Witness to the Gospel: The Theology of Acts*. Grand Rapids: Eerdmans, 1998.

MATSON, DAVID LERTIS. *Household Conversion Narratives in Acts: Pattern and Interpretation*. Journal for the Study of the New Testament Supplement Series 123. Sheffield: Sheffield Academic, 1996.

MATTHEWS, CHRISTOPHER R. *Philip: Apostle and Evangelist. Configurations of a Tradition*. Novum Testamentum Supplements 105. Leiden: Brill, 2002.

MATTHEWS, SHELLY. *First Converts: Rich Pagan Women and the Rhetoric of Mission in Early Judaism and Christianity*. Contraversions. Stanford: Stanford Univ. Press, 2001.

MOESSNER, DAVID P., editor. *Luke the Interpreter of Israel*. Volume 1: *Jesus and the Heritage of Israel: Luke's Narrative Claim upon Israel's Legacy*. Harrisburg, Pa.: Trinity, 1999.

MOUNT, CHRISTOPHER. *Pauline Christianity: Luke–Acts and the Legacy of Paul*. Novum Testamentum Supplements 104. Leiden: Brill, 2002.

NEYREY, JEROME H., editor. *The Social World of Luke–Acts: Models for Interpretation*. Peabody, Mass.: Hendrickson, 1991.

OMERZU, HEIKE. *Der Prozess des Paulus: Eine exegetische und rechtshistorische Untersuchung der Apostelgeschichte.* Beihefte zur Zeitschrift für die neutestamentliche Wissenschaft 115. Berlin: de Gruyter, 2002.

PERVO, RICHARD I. *Profit with Delight: The Literary Genre of the Acts of the Apostles*. Philadelphia: Fortress Press, 1987.

———. *Luke's Story of Paul*. Minneapolis: Fortress Press, 1990.

PLÜMACHER, ECKHARD. *Lukas als hellenistischer Schriftsteller: Studien zur Apostelgeschichte*. Studien zur Umwelt des Neuen Testaments 9. Göttingen: Vandenhoeck & Ruprecht, 1972.

REIMER, ANDY M. *Miracle and Magic: A Study in the Acts of the Apostles and the* Life of Apollonius of Tyana. Journal for the Study of the New Testament Supplement Series 235. London: Sheffield Academic, 2002.

SCHREIBER, STEFAN. *Paulus als Wundertäter: Redaktionsgeschichtliche Untersuchungen zur Apostelgeschichte und den authentischen Paulusbriefen*. Beihefte zur Zeitschrift für die neutestamentliche Wissenschaft 79. Berlin: de Gruyter, 1996.

SOFFE, GRAHAME. 'Christians, Jews and Pagans in the Acts of the Apostles.' In *Pagan Gods and Shrines of the Roman Empire,* edited by Martin Henig and Anthony King, 239–56. Oxford University Committee for Archaeology Monograph 8. Oxford University Committee for Archaeology, 1986.

SPENCER, F. SCOTT. *The Portrait of Philip in Acts: A Study of Roles and Relations*. Journal for the Study of the New Testament Supplement Series 67. Sheffield: Sheffield Academic, 1992.

STEGEMANN, WOLFGANG. *Zwischen Synagoge und Obrigkeit: Zur historischen Situation der lukanischen Christen*. Forschungen zur Religion und Literatur des Alten und Neuen Testaments 152. Göttingen: Vandenhoeck & Ruprecht, 1991.

STENSCHKE, CHRISTOPH W. *Luke's Portrait of Gentiles Prior to Their Coming to Faith*. Wissenschaftliche Untersuchungen zum Neuen Testament 2/108. Tübingen: Mohr/Siebeck, 1999.

STERLING, GREGORY E. *Historiography and Self-definition: Josephos, Luke–Acts, and Apologetic Historiography.* Novum Testamentum Supplements 64. Leiden: Brill, 1992.

TALBERT, CHARLES H., *Literary Patterns, Theological Themes and the Genre of Luke–Acts.* Society of Biblical Literature Monograph Series 20. Missoula, Mont.: Scholars, 1974.

——, editor. *Luke–Acts: New Perspectives from the Society of Biblical Literature Seminar.* New York: Crossroad, 1984.

——, editor. *Perspectives on Luke–Acts.* Edinburgh: T&T Clark, 1978.

TANNEHILL, ROBERT C. *The Narrative Unity of Luke–Acts: A Literary Interpretation.* Volume 2: *The Acts of the Apostles.* Foundations and Facets. Minneapolis: Fortress Press, 1990.

TAYLOR, JUSTIN. *Les Actes des deux Apôtres.* Volume 5: *Commentaire historique (Act. 9,1—18,22).* Études bibliques 23. Paris: Lecoffre, 1994.

THORNTON, CLAUS-JÜRGEN. *Der Zeuge des Zeugen: Lukas als Historiker der Paulusreisen.* Wissenschaftliche Untersuchungen zum Neuen Testament 56. Tübingen: Mohr/Siebeck, 1991.

TREMEL, B. 'Voie du salut et religion populaire: Paul et Luc face au risqué de paganisation.' *Lumen Vitae* 30/153–154 (1981) 87–108.

TYSON, JOSEPH B., editor. *Luke–Acts and the Jewish People: Eight Critical Perspectives.* Minneapolis: Augsburg, 1988.

WALASKAY, PAUL W. *'And so we came to Rome': The Political Perspective of St. Luke.* Society of New Testament Studies Monograph Series 49. Cambridge: Cambridge Univ. Press, 1983.

WILDHABER, BRUNO. *Paganisme populaire et prédication apostolique: D'après l'exégèse de quelques séquences des Actes: Eléments pour une théologie lucanienne de la mission.* Le monde de la Bible. Geneva: Labor et Fides, 1987.

WILSON, STEPHEN G. *The Gentiles and the Gentile Mission in Luke–Acts.* Society for New Testament Studies Monograph Series 23. Cambridge: Cambridge Univ. Press, 1973.

——. *Luke and the Law.* Society for New Testament Studies Monograph Series 50. Cambridge: Cambridge Univ. Press, 1983.

——. *Related Strangers: Jews and Christians, 70–170 C.E.* Minneapolis: Fortress Press, 1995.

WINTER, BRUCE W., editor. *The Book of Acts in Its First Century Setting.* 6 vols. Grand Rapids: Eerdmans, 1993–.

WITHERINGTON, BEN III, editor. *History, Literature, and Society in the Book of Acts.* Cambridge: Cambridge Univ. Press, 1996.

WOODS, EDWARD J. *The 'Finger of God' and Pneumatology in Luke–Acts.* Journal for the Study of the New Testament Supplement Series 205. Sheffield: Sheffield Academic, 2001.

3. *History of Religion*

ANKARLOO, BENGT, and STUART CLARK, editors. *Witchcraft and Magic in Europe: Ancient Greece and Rome.* Philadelphia: Univ. of Pennsylvania Press, 1999.

AUNE, DAVID E. 'Magic in Early Christianity.' In *Aufstieg und Niedergang der römischen Welt* 2.23.2 (1980) 1507–57.

BETZ, HANS DIETER, editor. *The Greek Magical Papyri, including the Demonic Spells.* 2d ed. Chicago: Univ. of Chicago Press, 1996.

———. *Antike und Christentum: Gesammelte Aufsätze 4.* Tübingen: Mohr/ Siebeck, 1998.

BURKERT, WALTER. 'Itinerant Diviners and Magicians: A Neglected Element in Cultural Contacts.' In *The Greek Renaissance of the Eighth Century B.C.: Tradition and Innovation,* edited by Robin Hägg, 115–19. Lund: Aströms, 1983.

CIRAOLA, LEDA, and JONATHAN SEIDEL, editors. *Magic and Divination in the Ancient World.* Ancient Magic and Divination 2. Leiden: Brill, 2002.

DAXELMÜLLER, CHRISTOPH. *Zauberpraktiken: Eine Ideengeschichte der Magie.* Zurich: Artemis & Winkler, 1993.

DICKIE, MATTHEW W. *Magic and Magicians in the Greco-Roman World.* New York: Routledge, 2001.

FARAONE, CHRISTOPHER A. 'Binding and Burying the Forces of Evil: The Defensive Use of 'Voodoo Dolls' in Ancient Greece.' *Classical Antiquity* 10 (1991) 165–220.

———. 'Molten Wax, Split Wine and Mutilated Animals: Sympathetic Magic in Near Eastern and Early Greek Oath Ceremonies.' *Journal of Hellenic Studies* 113 (1993) 60–80.

———, and DIRK OBBINK. *Magika Hiera: Ancient Greek Magic and Religion.* Oxford: Oxford Univ. Press, 1991.

GRADEL, ITTAI, *Emperor Worship and Roman Religion.* Oxford Classical Monograph. Oxford: Clarendon Press, 2002.

GRAF, FRITZ. *Magic in the Ancient World.* Translated by Franklin Philip. Revealing Antiquity 10. Cambridge: Harvard Univ. Press, 1997. French ed. 1994.

JANOWITZ, NAOMI. *Magic in the Roman World: Pagans, Jews, and Christians.* Religion in the First Christian Centuries. London: Routledge, 2001.

JORDAN, DAVID R., et al., editors. *The World of Ancient Magic: Papers from the First International Samson Eitrem Seminar at the Norwegian Institute at Athens 4-8 May 1997.* Papers from the Norwegian Institute at Athens 4. Bergen: Norwegian Institute at Athens, 1999.

KLAUCK, HANS-JOSEF. *The Religious Context of Early Christianity.* Translated by Brian McNeil. Minneapolis: Fortress Press, 2003 [2000].

KLAUCK, HANS-JOSEF. *Religion und Gesellschaft im frühen Christentum: Neutestamentliche Studien.* Wissenschaftliche Untersuchungen zum Neuen Testament 152. Tübingen: Mohr/Siebeck, 2003.

——, and B ALBETTE BÄBLER, *Dion von Prusa: Olypmische Rede oder Über die erste Erkenntnis Gottes.* 2d ed. Scripta Antiquitatis Posterioris ad Ethicam Religionemque pertinentia 2. Darmstadt: Wissenschaftliche Buchgesellschaft, 2002.

LUCK, GEORG. *Ancient Pathways and Hidden Pursuits: Religion, Morals, and Magic in the Ancient World.* Ann Arbor: Univ. of Michigan Press, 1999.

——. *Arcana Mundi: Magic and the Occult in the Greek and Roman Worlds: A Collection of Ancient Texts.* Baltimore: Johns Hopkins Univ. Press, 1985.

——. *Magie und andere Geheimlehren in der Antike.* Kröners Taschenausgabe 489. Stuttgart: Kröner, 1990.

MEYER, MARVIN, and PAUL MIRECKI, editors. *Ancient Magic and Ritual Power.* Religions in the Graeco-Roman World 129. Leiden: Brill, 1995.

MIRECKI, PAUL, and MARVIN MEYER. *Magic and Ritual in the Ancient World.* Religions in the Graeco-Roman World 141. Leiden: Brill, 2002.

NOCK, ARTHUR DARBY. *Essays on Religion and the Ancient World.* 2 vols. Cambridge: Harvard Univ. Press, 1972.

PREISENDANZ, K., and A. HENRICHS. *Papyri Graecae Magicae:Die griechischen Zauberpapyri.* 2 vols. 2d ed. Sammlung wissenschaftlicher Commentare. Stuttgart: Teubner, 1973–74.

PRICE, S. R. F. *Religions of the Ancient Greeks.* Key Themes in Ancient History. Cambridge: Cambridge Univ. Press, 1999.

——. *Rituals and Power: The Roman Imperial Cult in Asia Minor.* Cambridge: Cambridge Univ. Press, 1984.

THEE, FRANCIS C. R. *Julius Africanus and the Early Christian View of Magic.* Hermeneutische Untersuchungen zur Theologie 19. Tübingen: Mohr/Siebeck, 1984.

INDEX